Essentials of Medical Astrology

Harry F. Darling, M.D.

ISBN: 0-86690-004-7
LCC: 80-70672

Current Printing: 2004

Cover Design: Jack Cipolla

Published by:
American Federation of Astrologers, Inc.
6535 S. Rural Road
Tempe AZ 85283.

Printed in the United States of America

Dedicated

to Bev

Contents

Preface

It is both a pleasure and a privilege to be asked to write in behalf of Essentials of Medical Astrology for Harry F. Darling, M.D., PMAFA. As a good personal friend, former house guest, correspondent and colleague, I learned that Dr. Darling was born at Dorchester, Massachusetts on March 22, 1919. Both his father and his uncle were physicians.

As our friendship developed over the years, I found him to be most intelligent, understanding, compassionate and outstanding in a one-to-one relationship. The reader is given the opportunity in these pages to share the benefit of his special talent.

Dr. Darling is one among the few genuine medical astrologers in the United States. He is qualified as a physician and psychiatrist, as well as being an experienced professional astrologer. This is a rare combination to find anywhere because it demands the complete mastery of several unusual disciplines. Dr. Darling, with his medical education, has enjoyed the learning experience with famous astrology teachers, well-known professionals within the astrological community.

For example, Dr. Darling studied under Laurel Lowell. He authored *Organum Quarternii* and was further encouraged in its publication by Sylvia DeLong. Another book, entitled *Astropsychiatry*, was co-authored with Ruth Hale Oliver. In addition to his writing ind daily work as a psychiatrist, Dr. Darling enjoys the hobbies of metal and wood crafts, plus mosaics. He currently resides in the Ozark hills of Missouri with his wife, Bev. Professionally, Dr. Darling is board certified in homeopathy and is a professional member of the American Federation of Astrologers.

All of this is reinforced by his own experience, private study, and investigative research over a number of decades. Therefore, the good doctor is eminently qualified to bring the reader a number of very unique concepts. These concepts make this book a beacon light for your bookshelf. Compared with futile attempts by others to present medical astrology in broad, easy terms, Dr. Darling presents a fresh background and judiciously avoids any form of plagiarism of the others, either wittingly or unwittingly. Dr. Darling has carefully skirted this trap with a prudently prepared bibliography. Too many of the ancient writings have been copied and re-copied for centuries, which proves very frustrating to the serious student. Dr. Darling gives a most refreshing, informative, original and interesting presentation based upon personal experience–truly the best method.

In order to understand clearly defined techniques of basic delineation, the astrologer need only be versed in standard tropical astrology; from these the reader can go on to advanced methods as desired in the same terms. There are many example cases, copiously illustrated with charts. This text is useful both for the reader who wants to understand the basics of the subject and for the professional who wants to delve more deeply into it. The reader will reap a satisfaction here not found in any other volume on this topic. In passing, it might be mentioned that the material is comprehensive and generalized. The book, *Seventy-Five Windows*, rather specializes in a phase of medical astrology by offering 250 clinical cases of hypoglycemia and an emphasis on polarity and medical ethics. By contrast, Dr. Darling's work falls into a more broad classification in that it is truly comprehensive and has a wider appeal.

Dr. Darling has distinguished himself by presenting the reader with several unique features such as specific rulerships for each organ, endocrine gland, exogenous gland, muscle, tendon and ligament; the 10 cranial nerves (motor and sensory); the skull's interior structures; organs of special sense; the nerve roots of the spinal cord; sin and cutaneous nerves; and the autonomic nervous system. He has given benign planetary rulership; adverse planetary rulership; basic principles of delineation (a gem because of its original features and combinations); and the importance of fixed stars and solstice points in medical astrology.

In conclusion, this book is singularly and outstandingly unparalleled by any other such volume on the market today. Dr. Darling has thoroughly modernized medical astrology and left the Dark Ages trailing behind. Even very recent texts are invalid and outmoded by comparison in our mutual opinion and are the victims of the writer's trap.

Dr. Darling's style and presentation are easy reading as well as a valuable reference. *Essentials of Medical Astrology* should be on the bookshelf of every zealous astrologer concerned with this subject since it is the greatest boon to medical astrology in thousands of years.

Dr. F. Sims Pounds, Jr., LPMAFA, FAFA

x

Foreword

In preparing and writing this book, the question before me was always, what is essential?

From the medical standpoint, the basic sciences of anatomy and physiology are essential. William Davidson has modernized the latter (6), but astrological anatomy has not, with the exception of some observations by Davidson and by F. Sims Pounds (21), and a few articles in astrological journals here and there by physicians, materially changed since long before the time of Ptolemy. Astrology has lacked anatomy.

Davidson points out that the signs of the zodiac correspond with the structure of the body, the anatomy, and that the planets correspond with the functions, the physiology. I hold to that distinction and I firmly believe, on the basis of years of practice and research, that Davidson in this respect accomplished the breakthrough that made modern medical astrology possible.

What could be more natural? We divide the celestial zodiac into signs, and in mundane astrology we also divide the earth into signs and consider the physical influences on the zodiacal zones on the earth to be synchronous with planetary phenomena in earthquake and weather prediction. So, when an astrologer states that the liver is ruled by Jupiter, he is actually telling us the liver is in the sign of Sagittarius, which is ruled by the planet

Jupiter. This distinction has enabled me to devise a systematic astrological anatomy giving the zodiacal correspondences of the components of the various bodily anatomical systems.

An astrologer who has studied Silva Mind Control (27) or one of its numerous offshoots knows that human anatomy in general is an integral part of the course. Detailed anatomy can be learned much more easily in the alpha state than otherwise, and a diagrammatic atlas of anatomy in color, such is Barnes and Noble's, is the most graphic. In all probability, Ptolemy's "certain faculty" by means of which the astrologer is able to do good work is the ability to solve specific problems in the alpha state; fixation of the astrologer's attention on a horoscope triggers this state.

In the same way, anatomy may be applied to the reading of the horoscope for medical purposes. For purposes of physical and emotional well-being and personality growth, as well as occupational improvement and improved ability to adapt to one's environment, the Silva course is highly recommended. Silva accepts astrological influences as realities and believes they can be overcome by proper programming in the alpha state. It is safe, practical and free from philosophical and religious bias, which cannot necessarily be said of its many imitations.

As a result of using scientific anatomy I have found that lists of diseases are not only nonessential but also rather redundant. The stomach is in the sign of Cancer, for example; then it is redundant to state that gastritis, gastric ulcers, gastric cancer, achlorhydria or indigestion are under this sign. In order to know what is going on with the stomach, it is appropriate to look up the symptoms the patient or his astrologer tells you about in an appropriate medical reference. I use the *Merck Manual* as the best single reference, and more detailed texts only as necessary.

Speaking of lists, I have checked published lists of diseases that relate to certain planets in certain signs, and other lists of diseases that relate to two or more planets in certain single aspects, be they major or in midpoint relationship. I find them to be inaccurate and, therefore, worse than unessential.

Only a good knowledge of basic tropical astrology is essential for the practice of medical astrology. I rule out, therefore, two dozen or more systems and subsystems of astrology which are not basic tropical astrology; not on the ground that I do not believe in them, but rather because they are not essential to the system of medical astrology I practice and are not essential to 90 percent of astrologers. By basic tropical astrology I mean the system that uses major aspects; among these I include the quincunx and the contraparallel. I find these latter two aspects essential, as do several outstanding astrologers. Two of the most notable who have written about the quincunx are Frances Sakoian (25) and Barbara Watters (29). For a number of years I used Koch intermediate cusps as an alternative to Dalton; Watters told me that Dalton cusps were not Placidian, so it seems I had only thought I was converting from Placidian to Koch cusps. The AFA and other Astro-Numeric tables of intermediate Placidian cusps are the proper cusps to use; in my opinion they are superior to Koch and Dalton in accuracy.

Other than these the only thing I consider completely essential is the use of the Vertex; this is my only departure from the "norm" of the average American astrologer. I find it as essential as the quincunx for accurate work.

For the most part I omit minor aspects. Some systems of astrology emphasize them far more strongly than does the average astrologer, especially the semisquare and sesquiquadrate. One medical astrologer equates the orbs of these latter with those of major aspects, for example. I do, however, use minor aspects occasionally, but only when they are in close orb, as previously noted (4).

In terms of basic tropical astrology, chapter III, which follows anatomy and physiology, discusses basic principles of delineation. These principles are the bare essentials in my opinion, but I know from experience that very accurate medical astrology may be done using these and these alone.

Many astrologers want to learn more than basic methods and are drawn to minority schools, using their methods to supplement or to supersede basic tropical astrology. Sometimes they try to combine two different schools, and their work suffers because of the resultant hodge-podge. Fewer astrologers (and I am one of them) expend their learning and research in terms of standard tropical astrology. Hence, I have in chapter IV set down additional delineative methods. I advise the basic tropical astrologer initially to omit this chapter and references to these methods in the example cases in the second half of this book. Later, if desired, any new material the reader wants can be studied. I recommend solstices, stars and midpoints as the most often used additional material. To me they are essential at present even though they were not a decade ago when I started doing accurate medical astrology. I cannot do psychiatric astrology without midpoints. The reader will observe that psychiatry is specialty of medicine, whereas psychology is not. The latter probably can be done without midpoints because it is for the most part personality astrology embellished with complicated terminology and logorrhea. There are exceptions. Some astrologers who do excellent medical work do so with one-degree directions. I think secondary progressions give more information, so I remain with them.

Pounds has discussed the ethical and legal implications of medical astrology (21). I would add that in civil law jurisdictions (Louisiana, Quebec), malpractice is based on diagnosis.

Tissue or cell salts have for decades been equated with zodiacal signs and recently have been equated with planets. They are only 12 out of several hundred homeopathic remedies and should be prescribed only by a homeotherapist. I do not believe the medical astrologer can or should prescribe by the chart; in my opinion this is astro-quackery. The equation of Sun signs with herbs or of the planets with vitamins or minerals is purely speculative. At our present stage of knowledge I do not think it is the medical astrologer's role to prescribe on the basis of astrological findings. If regular medicine is not properly working and needs supplementation or replacement by alternative systems of medicine, this deficiency can be pointed out by the astrologer, who should be careful to note that the alternative systems are mentioned only as a matter of information.

After the completion of this manuscript, Dr. Margaret Millard's book on medical astrology was published. Her cases are interesting and informative and her technique inventive.

Harry F. Darling, M.D.

I

Anatomy

The first book I bought on medical astrology told me that the mandible formed a joint with the occiput. I could not figure how, if my lower jaw went way back there, I could eat without munching on my ears. For some months after reading that statement I had recurring dreams that I was chewing my ears ragged.

The book also told me that my upper jaw was in Aries and my lower jaw was in Taurus. Neither by means of natal, progressed nor transiting astrological phenomena could I figure out how I could have cavitation and gingivitis in both jaws—it was astrologically impossible. According to a more recent author the Sun must be natally in both these signs in order that dental troubles may occur in both jaws. So perhaps we have a double Sun.

The alleged causes of disease were remarkable. In one case, congenital tuberculosis was caused by a parent's gonorrhea. Barbara Watters points out (29) that Cornell, the physician-astrologer who wrote the *Encyclopedia of Medical Astrology*, considered diabetes mellitus to be a psychosis. I wonder if he committed severe cases to state hospitals.

I investigated medical astrology further and found that I had three livers in my natal chart: one was in the fifth genethliacal house in Sagittarius, the second was in the solar ninth house of Sagittarius and the third was the planet Jupiter. This was reassuring—I probably wouldn't die of cirrhosis, at least until after I had used up two of the livers. After considerable investigation into the literature I concluded that three livers would not, in fact, be enough. The pursuit of medical astrology would surely drive me to drink to the point of ruination of all three livers, and cirrhosis wasn't such a far-fetched idea after all. It had become quite clear that the eleventh commandment of medical astrology was "thou shalt not be lucid." So I quit medical astrology.

Then some years later Charles A. Jayne, Jr., sent me William Davidson's lectures on the subject (6). The material was scant but it made sense, because the anatomy was modern (circa 1950), and Davidson was five centuries ahead of much of anything I had previously read or even heard about.

During the past nine years following Davidson I have worked out in more detail a system of astrological anatomy and, as he advised, *confined anatomy entirely to the signs of the zodiac.* The reader is advised to ignore entirely such planetary rulerships as the Sun for the heart, for example. The heart, or at least the muscular portion, is in the sign Leo, which in turn is ruled by the Sun. But since *the ruler of the sign is not the sign itself,* the Sun may or may not relate to cardiac disturbance, depending on the particular chart. The Sun may or may not relate to the sign it occupies; it may or may not be significant of a cardiac or other illness. This distinction avoids confusion; anatomy and structure relate to the signs, whereas physiology and function relate to the planets. For example the adrenal medulla is structurally under Aries, but its secretion, adrenalin, is under Mars.

In the science of anatomy, which includes embryology and

2

comparative anatomy, the body is considered in terms of systems—musculo-skeletal, respiratory, digestive, genital-urinary, circulatory and neurological primarily, as well as organs of the special senses and endocrine glands. Each system develops in a different manner from the embryonic endodenn, mesoderm and ectoderm. Each system is consecutively considered from the head to tile tail—embryologically the terms are cephalad and caudad (the latter is the vestigal coccyx in the human being)—and feet.

Traditional zodiacal sign rulerships, which have not significantly changed since Manilius defined them about the time of Christ, do not take into account the fact that the signs are alternately positive and negative; alternately hard, unyielding and active; soft, yielding and passive. The positive signs correspond with the tissues which have to do with fight/flight, and the negative ones with those tissues which sustain and nourish the organism. In each bodily system there is consecutive arrangement of the signs from head to tail and feet, but the continuity is positive—Aries, Gemini, Leo, etc.—or negative—Taurus, Cancer, Virgo, etc.—within each system or subsystem. Bones and muscles, for example, are in positive signs, whereas joints are in negative ones; the thoracic organs are primarily in positive signs since they have to do with activity and the expenditure of energy, whereas the abdominal viscera have to do with sustaining and nourishing the organism and are primarily in negative signs.

The Skeletal System

Bones are synchronous with positive signs, and joints with negative ones. Bursae are anatomically related to joints and are under the sign of the joints with which they are interrelated. Not only are joint capsules in negative signs, but also their contents, the ligaments and, in vertebral joints and the knees, the joint

Table 1. The Bones and Joints

Positive Signs	*Negative Signs*
Aries—Skull, mandible, ossicles, and teeth (except Pulp). Cartilages of ear and nose.	*Taurus*—Mandibulotemporal joints and open fontanelles in infancy. Pulp of teeth. Cranial sinus linings. Cervical vertebral Joints.
Gemini—Cervical vertebrae; bones of shoulder girdle and upper extremity; claviculo-acromial joint.	*Cancer*—Sternoclavicular joints and joints of upper extremities.
Leo—Thoracic vertebrae, ribs and sternum. Articulations between ribs and Sternum.	*Virgo*—Thoracic vertebral and costo-vertebral joints.
Libra—Lumbar vertebrae.	*Scorpio*—Lumbar joints, including lumbosacral, and hip joint.
Sagittarius—Ilium, pubis including pubic joint, sacrum and sacroiliac joints; patella.	*Capricorn*—Knee joints includ-(ing prepatellar bursa but not patella, which is part of tendon of quadriceps femoris).
Aquarius—Ischium, tibia, fibula, bones of ankles and feet. Synarthrosis.	*Pisces*—Ankle and foot joints.

cartilages. Cartilages other than those contained in joints, and unencapsulated joints wherein the bones are joined by cartilage and are relatively immobile (synarthrosis) are in positive signs. The astrological signs as they are associated with this system are listed in Table 1.

Skeletal Muscles

These include the tendons and are governed by the sign of the bone from which they originate. To find the sign of a muscle, look to the bone of its origin, not of its insertion. In the case of a few larger muscles, the origin may be in multiple signs.

The pulmonary diaphragm is under Leo except for that portion which arises from lumbar vertebrae, which is under Libra.

The urogenital diaphragm is under both Sagittarius and Aquarius, inserting from both the pubic and ischial bones.

The patella is a sesamoid bone within the tendon of the quadriceps femoris, which originates from Sagittarius bones; the tendon, including the patella, is governed by the muscle's sign of origin.

The Respiratory System

Both the upper (trachea, larynx) and lower (lungs) respiratory systems are under Gemini, including the ciliated linings of the bronchi. The pleurae are serous membranes, under Cancer.

The Circulatory System

The Heart—The circulatory system undergoes more change in the embryo than does any other system, and the heart is no exception. At first it is a loop of vein with involuntary (negative sign) muscle. It develops into a highly complex semi-voluntary mechanism with striated muscle (positive sign); this is why the muscle of the heart is under Leo. Davidson puts the endocardium and valves under Cancer; the pericardium is under this sign also. The neurological tissues within the heart are in Aquarius.

Pulmonary Artery—The aortic arch and the thoracic aorta, like the heart, are under Leo; their linings are under Cancer. The abdominal aorta is under Libra; its lining is under Virgo.

Coronary Artery—The coronary artery supplies the heart muscle and is under Leo; the lining is under Cancer.

Other Arteries—Other arteries follow the same general pattern and are usually in the same sign as the muscles in which they lie; their linings are sub-ruled by negative signs.

Veins—Veins are all in negative signs, with the exception of the greater and lesser saphenous, which are just under the skin and are in Sagittarius and Aquarius respectively and are lined by Capricorn and Pisces respectively. The veins of the portal system are variously in Virgo or Scorpio and drain organs in these signs.

The Spleen—In one sense the spleen is analogous to the heart in that it pumps lymph, but the pumping is irregular and the muscle is not striated. It derives from a duodenal bud and is a composite organ, under Virgo because of its derivation, and ruled also by Libra as it relates to the blood and lymphatic systems.

The Lymphatics—Lymphatics are in the same negative sign as are the associated veins.

The Digestive System

Under Taurus are the salivary glands, the mucous membrane lining the mouth, including the lips, fauces, tonsils and pharynx; the mucous membrane covering the tongue is in Taurus.

Under Cancer is the stomach, including the pyloric valve.

Under Virgo are the peritoneum, omentum, small intestine, the gallbladder and associated ducts.

Like the spleen, the liver derives from a duodenal bud and is under Virgo, but it is also under Sagittarius because it also derives from the embryonic mesoderm. (Probably this is the reason the liver and arterial blood are associated with Jupiter, as it relates to blood formation along with bone marrow in positive signs. Jupiter is one of its rulers, and Mercury is the other as relates to its function, but anatomically this .complex composite gland is under Virgo and Sagittarius.)

Also derived from the duodenum and under Virgo are the pancreas and its duct. It is another composite gland, and the Islets of Langerhans, which secrete insulin, are under Taurus.

Under Scorpio is the large intestine (which includes the rectum and internal sphincter of the anus—the external sphincter is under Aquarius because it is a voluntary muscle), the cecum, and vermiform appendix.

The Genito-Urinary System

No less than twice do changes occur in the kidney in the mammalian embryo after it first develops. As a result, the vascular medulla of the kidney is under Libra, whereas the remainder of the organ is under Scorpio, as are the bladder, ureters, urethra, and the involuntary sphincter; the voluntary sphincter is under Aquarius.

The ovaries, Fallopian tubes, uterus, and vagina are under Scorpio, as are the external genitalia that are covered by mucous membrane. The mons pubis, however, is covered by skin and is under Sagittarius. In pregnancy the female genital system is also under Cancer—the corpus luteum, fetal membrane, and placenta.

Analogous male organs do not differ from the female except that while the testes are in Scorpio they are covered by skin, so the skin of the penis and the scrotum are in Sagittarius and Aquarius respectively; the glans penis and lining of the prepuce are membranous and in Scorpio.

The breast is generally under Cancer, although the overlying skin is in Leo. The nipple and areola are mucous membrane, rather than skin, and are under Scorpio; Paget's disease of the breast and some other relatively rare conditions are under Scorpio, although mammary carcinoma is ordinarily under Cancer.

The Endocrines

Neither the anatomy nor the physiology of the endocrine glands is entirely defined scientifically; neurohormones in particular tend to change every few years. Certain cells within the brain, which are evidently located in Arien, Taurean and Geminian areas, secrete various neurohormones which are physiologically characterized as having the qualities of Mars, Venus and Mercury respectively. Emotional correlates of illnesses related functionally to Mars and Venus have been intensively researched astrologically by Ruth Hale Oliver (18); correlates of Venus and Mercury will be published elsewhere. Neurohormones come from cells that are not consolidated sufficiently to be classified as separate glandular organs.

The practice of relegating an endocrine gland to each zodiacal sign has no basis in anatomical fact. Three or four neurohormones in the brain, as well as hypertensive renin, is secreted from cells located near the glomeruli of the kidneys; and the Islets of Langerhans within the pancreas are separate isolated areas disseminated within a gland, rather than being a separate gland. At least half a dozen hormones are secreted from cells that are not glands. The glandular system relates primarily to the autonomic nervous system, with the exception of digestive secretions, which relate to the gastro-intestinal system and cerebral neurohormones, as follows: The adrenal medulla is in Aries. The thyroid gland, the thymus gland, and the pineal gland are all in Taurus. The pineal gland is regarded with religious awe by many astrologers, either as the seat of the Ajna chakra or as the actual seat of spiritual development, the third eye of psychic awareness; Anatomically it reaches its greatest development before puberty, and the glandular tissue is gradually replaced by connective tissue after puberty. If prior to puberty the pineal gland is destroyed, puberty ensues prematurely with full sexual development even in small children. I do not want to tread on the religious toes of any reader, but the pineal gland belongs in Taurus as opposition the gonads in Scorpio; when it declines in action, puberty ensues. Much the same process occurs with the thymus gland, which is also temporary and gradually disappears after puberty.

The suprarenals are in Cancer. The juxtaglomerular cells and the anterior pituitary gland are in Scorpio. The posterior pituitary gland is in Sagittarius. As Davidson points out, the anterior and posterior pituitary glands are two separate glands under two separate signs, and they have two separate primary functions.

The parathyroids are under Aquarius. They regulate voluntary muscle tone, and as such the two rulers of this sign fit the parathyroid secretion nicely. Saturn is slow, and Uranus is vibratory and spasmodic. The reader will note that these glands, the thyroid and the thymus, all differentiate from contiguous embryonic tissues.

Organs of Special Sense

The Nose—The olfactory receptor cells are in Taurus and are part of the olfactory nerve; as such they are the only part of the brain that is completely external. ("Smelling out" a situation means intuiting it, so if there is any vestigal third eye, it is these cells.) The olfactory mucous membrane is in Scorpio, opposite Taurus, and merges into the nasal mucous membrane in Taurus (which is continuous with the membranes lining the sinuses in the same sign). The bones and cartilage of the nose are in Aries.

The Eye—The retina, in Taurus, is the end of the optic nerve; the associated visual purple is more chemical than anatomical and is under the planet Uranus. The eyeball and associated muscles are in Aries, as is the iris. Clear structures are in Aquarius; in the eye these are the cornea and the lens. Again chemical, the clear fluid contents of the eyeball are under Uranus. The conjunctiva and the entire lachrymal system are under Taurus.

The Ear—The external ear is under Aries, and this includes the cartilage and drum. The middle ear is under Taurus, as is the auditory tube. The ossicles, however, are under Aries. The chorda tympani are under Taurus. The osseous labyrinth is under Aries, whereas the membranous labyrinth is under Taurus. The fluid contents of the semicircular canals are under Aquarius.

The Tongue—The musculature, naturally, is under the double sign of Gemini. The membranous exterior and sensory receptors of the tongue are under Taurus.

The Nervous System

From the standpoint of trauma the brain may generally be considered to be under Aries. The meninges and arteries of the brain are all under this sign. The venous sinuses and ventricular linings of the brain are under Taurus; the clear fluid filling the ventricles is physiological and under Uranus.

The *cerebrum* is under Aries, Taurus and Gemini. The corticocortical neuronal association systems, which have to do with thinking, are under Gemini. Using Netter's terminology (17), the somato-motor and suppressor areas are under Aries; whereas the olfactory, somato-sensory and visuo-sensory areas are under Taurus. Effector pathways, those that send impulses from the brain to the body and their nuclei, are under Aries, whereas affector pathways and nuclei are under Taurus.

The *cerebellum* is under Aries and Taurus. It receives (afferent, Taurus) proprioceptive, optic, acoustic, touch and vestibular impulses, acting as a balancing center and relay station regulating the postural and dynamic conditions of the body. Efferents and afferents are respectively in Aries and Taurus; there may be some cortical fibers under Gemini. (The functional anatomy of the cerebrum is not too clear; there is some question in my mind as to whether the kinesthetic and equilibrium functions may be partly under Aquarius along with the organ of balance. Further evidence is needed, both medical and astrological.)

Much of the rest of the brain can be considered by systems, tracts and associated nuclei in the same signs. Nuclei govern the tracts concerned; for example, the nuclei of the optic nerve are under Taurus, and so is the entire tract up to and including the retina. Some cranial nerves are motor and sensory and should be considered separately, with motor nuclei and tracts under Aries or Gemini, and sensory nuclei and tracts under Taurus. The cranial nerves are listed in Table 2, with their motor functions and sensory functions separate. The autonomic function of the vagus will be considered later.

The *medulla spinalis* is a continuation of the medulla oblongata, with its meninges under positive signs correspond-

11

Table 2. Cranial Nerves

Motor	Sensory
Aries	*Taurus*
	I. Olfactory
	II. Optic
III. Oculomotor	
IV. Trochlear	
V. Trigeminal motor	V. Trigeminal sensory
VI. Abducens	
VII. Facial motor	VII. Facial sensory
	VIII. Acoustic
Gemini	
IX. Glossopharyngeal (to pharynx and stylopharyngeal muscle)	IX. Glossopharyngeal sensory
X. Vagus (to base of tongue, larynx, pharynx)	
XI. Spinal accessory	
XII. Hypoglossal	

Table 3. Nerve Roots of the Spinal Cord

Segments	Motor	Sensory
C 1	Aries	Taurus
C 2, 3	Gemini	Taurus/Cancer
C 4-8, T1	Gemini	Cancer
T 2-10	Leo	Virgo
T 11-12	Libra	Scorpio
L 1-5	Sagittarius	Capricorn
S 1-5, Cx	Aquarius	Pisces

ing with vertebrae. The nerve roots and associated areas of the cord are motor in positive signs and sensory in negative signs

Table 4. Skin Rulerships and Cutaneous Nerves

Segment	Cutaneous Nerves	Skin Rulerships
C 1-3	Taurus	Aries
C 4-8, T-1	Cancer	Gemini
T 2-10	Virgo	Leo
T 11-12	Scorpio	Libra
L 1-5	Capricorn	Sagittarius
S 1-5, Cx	Pisces	Aquarius

(see Table 3).

Dermal segments are slightly different in their segmentation (see Table 4).

Motor nerves can be followed a good deal more easily than sensory nerves, since they are in the same signs as the muscles they innervate. The segmental innervation of muscles is tabulated in anatomical texts. (Note that skin areas in positive signs are always sub-ruled by the succeeding negative sign, because there is always sensory innervation and a softer subdermal area.)

The Autonomic Nervous System

The sympathetic ganglia, which are contiguous to the spinal cord, are in the same positive signs as are the motor fibers of the nerve roots. Signs change in the various portions and plexuses, shown in Table 5, with corresponding, parasympathetics, principally the tenth (vagus) cranial nerve. Sympathetic nerves are in positive signs, parasympathetics in negative signs. Sign equivalents are approximate, but it should be remembered that in most instances more distal plexuses are contiguous to vessels. Phylogenetically, the autonomic nervous system precedes the central nervous system and so has acquired more aberrations as subsequent structures appeared around it.

Table 5. The Autonomic Nervous System

Sympathetic	Parasympathetic
Cephalic Portion	
Aries—Internal carotid nerves, sympathetic branches of vagus nerve	*Taurus*—Parasympathetic branches of oculomotor, facial, glossopharyngeal nerves; intracranial portion of parasympathetic branch of vagus nerve
Gemini—Sympathetic branches of spinal accessory, glossopharyngeal nerves	
Cervical Portion	
Aries—Superior cervical ganglion	
Gemini—Inferior cervical ganglion	
Thoracic Portion	
Leo—T 1-4 ganglia	*Cancer*—Cardiac and all respiratory branches of vagus
Leo—Celiac plexus	*Virgo*—Hepatic and pancreatic, small intestinal branches of vagus
Libra/Sagittarius—Inferior mesenteric ganglion	Scorpio—Colonic branch of vagus
Lumbosacral Portion	
Sagittarius—Hypogastric, pelvic vesical plexuses	*Scorpio*—Pelvic nerve
Aquarius—Vaginal and prostatic plexuses	

II

Physiology, Health and Disease

The reactivity of a given sign indicates both the manner and the intensity of reaction to disease. Gemini and the Fire signs react most intensely and most suddenly. Gemini is the fastest reactor. Aries is almost as fast and reacts more intensely. Consequently the incubation period of illness is faster when these two signs are concerned. Leo is a little slower and less intense than Aries, but it remains fixed and steady in the reaction, resisting illness strenuously. The reaction of Sagittarius is more fluctuating and less intense.

Libra reacts with the steadiness of Leo, but less intensely; indeed it is the least intense of the air signs. Aquarius reacts spasmodically and intermittently to illness, as intensely as Gemini at times and at other times so spasmodically as to be paralyzed in its effect and apparently non-reactive.

Of the negative signs, Taurus and Scorpio are the most intense reactors and, like Leo, steady and non-fluctuating in their defense against disease, slow and massive in their reaction. Scorpio is the more massive in reaction. As in mundane astrology, the fixed signs tend to be the strongest reactors, but they are not necessarily the fastest.

Virgo is steady but less intense than Taurus. Cancer reacts in much the same manner as does Virgo, except that the reaction is slowly alternating, ebbing and flowing between reaction and non-reaction. Cancer may appear not to react to disease at all, but it will slowly develop a fairly intense reaction and can overcome disease.

Capricorn and Pisces react the least intensely. What reaction Capricorn has is slow and steady. Pisces fluctuates between a Capricornian type of reaction and no reaction at all.

It is an over-generalization to state that the triplicities resist disease in order of fire, air, water and earth signs. It may, be said that, in general, positive signs attack disease, whereas negative signs resist it, as follows:

Attack	Resistance
Aries sudden total	Taurus active maximal
Gemini rapid total	Cancer intermittent moderate
Leo moderate subtotal	Virgo active moderate
Libra minimal subtotal	Scorpio sustained total
Sagittarius intermittent total	Capricorn active minimal
Aquarius intermittent rapid	Pisces intermittent minimal

Note that some negative signs resist illness more strongly than some positive signs attack it.

The reaction of the body to illness, the means by which the body combats it, is indicated traditionally by the natal Ascendant, its ruler and the planets in the first house. I tend on the basis of experience to adapt the mundane principles of catastrophic astrology; for example, earthquakes (28), wherein a male fire planet

16

or several planets conjunction, opposition or square angles are synchronous with the catastrophe. Just as some people look and react more like their Midheaven and tenth house, so sometimes is the reaction of the body to disease. If, for example, the Midheaven is more strongly, more malefically, aspected to the Ascendant in some individuals, so does the reaction to disease tend to be more characteristic of the Midheaven than of the Ascendant. This does not preclude, however, in such charts, a strong Ascendant reaction when the horizontal axis of the chart has progressions and transits to it. Conversely, when the Ascendant is the stronger but is not stimulated by progressions and transits, but the Midheaven is so stimulated, then the Midheaven, will react. One axis will react at one time of life and another at a different time because of selective stimulation by progression and transits.

When a planet is conjunction, square or quincunx an angle of the natal chart, its influence, more or less entirely supersedes the reaction of the zodiacal sign on the angular cusp because of its great intensity. This reaction is most intense when the planet concerned is a malefic one or is adversely aspected by a malefic. While it may supersede the sign to a great extent, it should not be forgotten that the ruler of the sign is still effective as an influence upon it, especially when the ruler is strong. There is less intensity when a malefic or a planet aspected by a malefic is in the angular house but not conjunction the cusp.

Each planet has its own physiologic reaction. The Sun is indicative of the vitality of the patient in general. If it is well aspected, the vitality is good. This is especially so when it is aspected to an angle, to the Moon, or to both.

A person might be vital and vigorous but also be prone to poor health and, conversely, a person might not be vital or vigorous but live to be more than 100 years old without having had a major illness. The Moon represents the health, and when it is well aspected (especially when it is well aspected to the Sun, to an angle, or to both), a person tends to be healthy. The viscera are, in general, sensitive to the influence of the Moon and its aspects in the natal chart. Gastric secretions relate physiologically with the Moon.

Older astrologers (23) taught that the health of the male was governed by the Sun, and that of the female by the Moon. While the male tends to be more muscular and long than the female, and the female to be more endomorphic in comparison, nonetheless in both sexes the general condition of the musculoskeletal system relates to the natal Sun, and that of the viscera to the Moon. The Sun determines generally the status of the catabolic organs, and the Moon the status of the anabolic organs, regardless of sex; their interrelationship and their relationships with the natal angles give a general description of the health, vitality and resistance to disease.

Mercury, like the Sun and Moon, is neither a benefic nor a malefic planet. It has a general relationship with the central nervous system in that it is regulatory; it has a balancing effect on the two branches of the autonomic nervous system.

Venus, the minor benefic, has a general influence over the parasympathetic branch of the autonomic nervous system, associated endocrines, and the sensory, afferent areas of the central nervous system. As a physiological influence, the corresponding neurohormones are under this planet, as are other endocrines.

The masculine malefics are Mars and Pluto. Davidson (6) describes Mars as hot, dry, inflammatory, infectious. When Mars is placed in a sign, afflicted, or when Mars afflicts a planet in a sign, there is a predisposition to infection and also to intense reactions to infection. Davidson calls Pluto a double or triple Mars, and Pluto is found when infections are massive—such as cellulitis and eroding infectious ulcers—and when these infections occur there is likely to be anatomical destruction of tissue, such as arthritis deformans, osteomyelitis, or gangrene.

Physiologically, Mars acts as a general stimulant to the autonomic nervous system and governs adrenalin specifically, the hormone that stimulates the mesodermally derived tissues. The hormones of the anterior pituitary gland and of the gonads are under both this planet and Pluto in their action.

The feminine malefic, Neptune, is as diffuse, surreptitious, insidious and weakening as in personality/psychological astrology. The chemicals in lymph and plasma are generally under Neptune's influence. Frequently, illnesses involving Neptune are asymptomatic. They are discovered only when far advanced, and frequently they are tumors and degenerative diseases. When Mars and Pluto are involved with Neptune, the illnesses are infectious in nature, chronic and very insidious in onset. With the neuter malefics, Saturn and Uranus, the diseases are degenerations, wasting diseases and tumors; with Mercury, the other neuter planet, this also occurs, but not quite as severely as a rule.

Saturn is hardening, concretizing and degenerating, and is related to tumor formation when adversely aspecting the Sun or Moon, much as is Neptune; but whereas Neptune relates to the dissemination of illness locally or generally, Saturn concretizes. Both planets, by themselves, are cold and relate to the noninfectious breakdown, stagnation, degeneration and production of tumors. Neither by itself is infectious except in combination with Mars or Pluto.

While Uranus and Saturn are both neuter malefics, they conflict when in combination, unlike the masculine malefics that only augment each other and the Sun. Together, they make for imbalance, particularly of the nervous system; difficulty with equilibrium, balance, kinesthetic sense, spasticity, spasm or hypotonia or an alternation of the two. Like Saturn, Uranus augments the effects of Mars and Pluto, as concerns infections, and augments Neptune and Saturn when degenerations and tumors are concerned. With Venus, the Sun or the Moon, Uranus is productive of imbalance, spasticity or hypotonia; many functional disorders of this kind are related to Uranus.

Jupiter is not necessarily a benefic planet medically, no more than it is mundanely. It is additive in action for better or for worse, will augment the action of any natal malefic; in adverse aspect a Jupiter transit can be detrimental.

Afflictions of Mars or Pluto to either the Sun or the Moon often indicate a propensity to infection in the sign the Sun or Moon is in or rules and indicate a general proneness to infection and a concomitant Martian type of reactivity to it. However, more than this single affliction by Mars is necessary to show more than average proneness to infection; multiple, more severe afflictions must be evident in the natal chart to denote proneness to moderate or severe illness, as a general rule. Both older and more modern literature notes the dire health consequences of Mars square Moon, for example—a theory to which I do not subscribe.

A sign will not be caused to react to disease unless a planet in it, or its significator, is afflicted by adverse aspect. This is because there is a certain normal physiology in each sign which, like life itself, has momentum—it continues to keep going until it is stopped, a sort of perpetual motion. The metabolism of each cell, each organ of the total human body, continues to go on as spontaneously as does that of the amoeba. This instinct for self-perpetuity is a quality shared by the least and the most specialized living organisms. Metabolism consists of both anabolism and katabolism. The anabolic organs derived from the embryologic endoderm take substances into the body and

20

prepare them for utilization; the katabolic organs derived from the embryologic ectoderm and mesoderm utilize what is prepared.

Carbohydrates, for example, are taken into the body, digested and converted into glycogen, which is stored in the liver, a complex anabolic process. When energy is needed, the glycogen is converted into energy and used, a katabolic process. Astrologically it may be said that positive signs are katabolic, and that negative signs are anabolic, but there is an overlap that increases with the degree of complexity and specialization of the organism. It may be more accurate to state as a generality that positive signs are concerned with fight/flight, when the entire musculoskeletal system, afferent nervous system lungs and heart (all in positive signs) are activated; when they are not activated, nature/nurture within the negative signs continue uninterruptedly. It is assumed that in the natural zodiac the signs remain in balance. Since, however, we do not live under the influence of the signs alone but also are under the influence of the planets, this assumption is only a generalization.

Usually when someone does not appear to know what he is talking or writing about, I pay little attention to him. Consequently, when astrologers write about tissue or cell salts and mean trace elements, or write about tissue or cell salts and mean mineral deficiencies, their conclusions are not to be greatly trusted. When in addition they show fanatic adherence to single schools or offshoots of medicine and promise 100 percent results, they are greatly not to be trusted. Conversely, too close adherence to very narrow definitions and practices of standard and regular (not allopathic, for this school has long since ceased to exist) medicine or astrology, or both, closes many doors to treatment.

I remember that my old friend Clarence Hines used to say of treatment that anything useful was good, and if it was not useful it was not good for the particular patient.

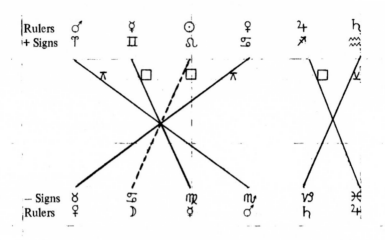

Figure 1. Major Aspects Between Signs and Rulers

A clue to the relationship between the signs and the planets may be found in the old rulers of the signs (omitting transaturnians).

Prior to the development of the mesoderm the lining of the neural groove is comprised of the negative signs successively from cephalad (head) to caudad (tail), and its exterior is comprised of the positive signs. Within either the positive or negative group only, the sextile and the trine are represented. The major aspects between positive and negative signs are the square and the opposition. Beginning caudad, Aries is ruled by Mars, quincunx Scorpio, which is also so ruled. Within the quincunxes the signs ruled by Mercury are square, as are those ruled by the Lights. Beyond the quincunx, to the right of the diagram in Figure 1, the signs ruled by Jupiter are square, and those ruled by Saturn are semisextile. This minor aspect is contiguous between positive signs and negative signs just before and after them; Taurus, negative, for example, adjoins, is semisextile and contiguous to the positive signs Aries and Gemini. Continuity of disease from Taurus to Aries is, for example, noted in sinusitis only when the periosteum and bone are invaded in severe cases, or when trauma to the vertebrae of the lower back (Libra) causes disc or other joint disease (Scorpio) in that area. But a sore throat or cold in the head (Taurus) can continue in the same sign as an ear infection or in the next sextile positive sign (Gemini) as laryngitis or bronchitis. Continuity again, among either positive or negative signs, goes with sextiles as, for example, emphysema (Gemini) and cardiac decompensation (Leo). Metastasis of infection or malignancy may relate to trines as cancer of the breast (Cancer) and the uterine cervix (Scorpio), or may relate to oppositions or squares of the quadratures, coronary disease (Leo), cardiac arrhythmia (Aquarius), sore throat (Taurus) and pyelitis (Scorpio), for example. Contiguity of illness is within the same sign. Continuity is semisextile or sextile. Metastasis relates to trines, squares and oppositions. Anatomically corresponding to the first eight signs, there is no bifurcation, but bifurcation starts with Sagittarius and Aquarius and is complete with the last two signs. Although there are upper extremities, Gemini is not bifurcated since the lungs touch; in the lower extremities, Sagittarius and Aquarius are not visceral.

Planets posited in signs alter them similarly to the quality of their mundane influences:

Moon	Benefic, viscerotonic
Mercury	Benefic, cerebrotonic
Sun	Benefic, somaticotonic
Venus	Benefic, viscerotonic

These planets are more influenced than influencing. If adversely aspected by malefics, the quality of the malefic will transmit its quality to the sign within which the benefic planet is posited.

Mars	strenuous, infectious
Jupiter	magnifying (intensifies actions of planet with which it is interrelated)

Saturn	proliferating (concretions, tumorfactions)
Uranus	spasmodic, explosive
Neptune	diffusing, insidious
Pluto	massively strenuous, infectious

If malefic planets are in adverse aspect, the degree of that adversity depends upon whether their embryologically related categories are mixed (the categories being masculine—mesomorphic, sthenic; feminine—endomorphic, pyknic; neuter—asthetic, ectomorphic). For example, Moon square Neptune is not especially malefic because both planets are feminine—endormorphic. Since Jupiter is both masculine and feminine, it mixes well with both groups; for example, Jupiter square Neptune or Pluto. Since Jupiter is not neuter, however, it is slightly more malefic square Mercury than square Moon or Sun, definitely malefic when adversely aspected to the neuter-ectomorphic malefics Saturn and Uranus.

Relatively benign relationships between planets despite adverse relationships are shown in Figure 2.

Adverse combinations in conjunction, square, opposition, parallel, quincunx and semisextile aspects (which Margaret Hone describes as not necessarily benefic) are shown in Figure 3.

A few aspects cannot be categorized precisely as either adverse or benign, especially Mercury-Jupiter and Mercury-Sun; it depends upon what planet or planets are associated with them.

Certain psychiatric conditions, wherein the malefic combinations are used in midpoint configurations, as in Ruth Oliver's research (3) on murder and: suicide (4) appear to be synchronous only with malefic groups. By no means, however can this be said of physical illnesses, wherein almost any combination of adverse planets, in adverse aspect or as related to midpoints;

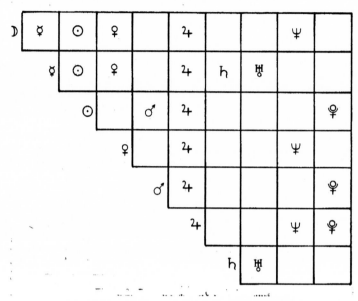

Figure 2. Benign Planetary Relationships
(table reads horizontally, left to right)

may correspond with a given illness. Combinations of Saturn and Uranus, for example, are as malefic as they are in mundane astrology, whereas they do not relate to midpoint complexes as they are used in psychiatric conditions. Jupiter in adverse aspect to any malefic is prone to accentuate the action of the latter, again as in mundane astrology.

Oliver discusses the more, benign configurations (11) as they relate to somatotypes (18). For example, in top baseball players she has studied, relating to Neptune conjunction Jupiter/Pluto, she states, "Here we find Neptune, an endormorphic planet, at a powerful mesomorphic midpoint, that of Jupiter (mellowness) and Pluto (strength) . . . Mars/Pluto, mesomorphic planet or Ascendant, turns up regularly in the charts of boxers. . . . There seems to be no doubt that the relaxed power of Jupiter/Pluto

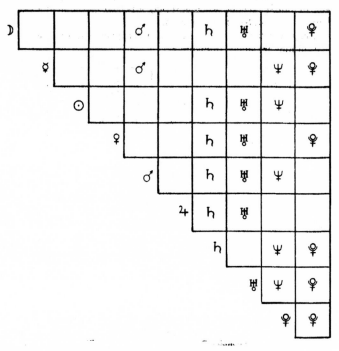

Figure 3. Adverse Planetary Combinations

conjunction Neptune is helpful for the great baseball player, and the powerful attack of Mars/Pluto conjunction mesomorphic planet or Ascendant for the great boxers" (see Chapter III, principle 12).

Planets within and integrated with the signs alter their reactivity. In terms of psychosomatic reactivity:

- The Moon is parasympathetic regulatory.
- The Sun is sympathetic regulatory.
- Mercury is regulatory of the cognitive areas of the central nervous system.
- Venus is parasympathetic stimulatory.

26

- Mars is sympathetic-psychomotor stimulatory.
- Jupiter is regulatory of the balance between the sympathetic and parasympathetic branches of the autonomic nervous system and stimulatory of either or both in that it augments the actions of male and female planets.
- Saturn is opposition in action to Jupiter, inhibitory generally of the autonomic nervous system and inhibitory of male and female planets.
- Uranus is parasympathetic inhibitory.
- Neptune is sympathetic inhibitory.
- Pluto is sympathetic stimulatory with much more intensity than Mars.

Balance, stimulation and inhibition are within certain normal limits of variation in physical type when beneficially aspected. When malefically aspected, the tissue corresponding to the sign or quadruplicity associated with the planet will have disease susceptibility.

III

Basic Principles of Delineation

The astrologer who has some knowledge of medicine should have no difficulty in equating modern natal chart anatomical locations as given in chapter I and in determining the basic physiological effects of the planets as given in chapter II. This is especially so when a case history of previous illnesses and a description of the present illness is compared with the chart. Since medicine is an art and science that has a vocabulary of some 20,000 words, it is not a matter of remembering what one has learned but rather of knowing where to look up what one does not know or remember, or knowing whom to ask.

The physician or other professional trained in the biological sciences who has come into astrology may well feel diffident about his astrological proficiency. He should be reassured that most astrologers (90 percent) use standard tropical astrology, the luminaries and only eight planets, Placidus cusps, secondary progressions and transiting planets. A decade ago I started doing medical astrology with these standard tools, plus the single (and simple) addition of the Vertex because it gave me more angular data. Be assured that with some knowledge of medicine and an adequate proficiency in basic astrology, it is possible to learn adequate medical astrology. What is more necessary than overly complex or overly detailed knowledge of either profession is what Ptolemy called "that certain faculty" by which the astrologer interprets the horoscope. Some call it intuition, but I prefer Harold Willey's term, "subliminal cues." The astrologer who has this faculty can become proficient; the astrologer who does not have it cannot become proficient because he cannot delve into his subconscious and, from an almost infinite number of variables, come up with the accurate and selective delineation which fits the case and explains it.

The influx within recent years of Ph.D.s from the social sciences into personality astrology has not been without benefit. At least one of them, highly placed in a prestigious university, however, teaches his students not to use this faculty but rather to use "reason," which means "going by the book," in his case a shelf full of his own volumes. I submit that the man is not an astrologer and is teaching his pupils not to be real astrologers because he does not have, or is inhibiting, the very faculty which is basic for the practice of this profession or of any other profession that involves direct personal contact with the human being. This paragraph is interpolated here as a warning to the student not to extinguish his interpretative faculty. The pseudo-intellectual explains everything by "reason" in order not to experience life itself—a motive generated by fear of such experience.

It is suggested that the reader skip the next chapter at first and also skip examples of special principles in subsequent chapters; this is for the reason that it is best to build a good frame of reference before elaborating upon its details.

30

Natal Principles

1. *An affliction of a given quadrature is an indication of potential illness which is anatomically related to any or all of the signs of the same quadrature.*

This is the foundation of medical astrology. The quadratures are as follows:

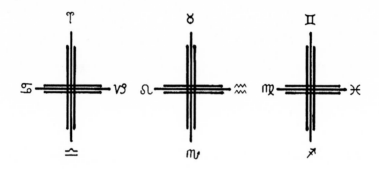

2. *An affliction to a sign's ruler indicates potential disturbance in the anatomical areas corresponding to the afflicted planet; do not omit the old rulers.*

Principle 1 pinpoints anatomy by quadrature; principle 2 pinpoints the particular sign involved. This does not mean that the ruling planet, or any other planet, equates with the sign anatomically; the worst trap in medical astrology is the belief that planets, as well as signs, are anatomical in nature. The old ruler of Scorpio is Mars; of Aquarius, Saturn; and of Pisces, Jupiter.

3. *Malefics which afflict angles or afflict other planets conjunction angles indicate the greatest susceptibility to illness in the quadrature concerned. This is first degree proneness to illness.*

In this principle, anatomy (principle 1) and physiology (principle 2) are combined at the angles so that the affliction is simulta-

31

neous and therefore more severe than separate anatomical and physiological afflictions. This principle is more reminiscent of the mundane astrology of natural catastrophes than it is of personality astrology, and anybody who has suffered or who has treated a catastrophic illness will tell you it is indeed a natural human disaster. Charts that are particularly afflicted genethliacally in this manner were called "earthquake charts" by Zane Harmon many years ago, and his terminology is certainly correct medically.

4. *When the affliction to the given quadrature is in angular houses but there are no planetary aspects to angles, the proneness to illness is moderate, or second degree: When the affliction is in succeedent or cadent houses and unaspected to angles, the proneness to illness is minimal, or third degree.*

It may be that an affliction in succeedent houses indicates slightly more proneness to illness than one in cadent houses, but this is a moot point.

5. *The Sun sign may not be relevant to proneness to illness at all, or to a particular illness at a given time.*

If the Sun is not afflicted, why should it be relevant? Yet, over the years, beginning with Paracelsus, astrologers have advocated herbs by Sun sign and more recently have advocated Schuessler's tissue salts, one for each sign. Schuessler's salts were long ago incorporated into homeopathic medicine; the physician gives them to his patient as the result of his examination of the patient and his evaluation of the symptoms, like any other homeopathic remedy. The Schuessler tissue salts corresponding with the patient's Sun sign may be contraindicated, useless and even harmful. Megavitamin therapy is similar. Oil-soluble vitamins are always potentially harmful, but even water-soluble vitamins can produce at least disturbing side effects. Due caution is advised. Due caution is also advised against yoga indiscriminately recommended for Sun signs.

6. The Sun is generally indicative of the patient's vitality, and the Moon of his general health. Their aspects to planets and angles both as to type and frequency will give an estimate of the patient's general hardiness and ability to withstand disease.

7. The most prominently aspected angle of the chart indicates the manner of resisting disease.

Personality astrology teaches us that the first house indicates the general health, appearance and temperament of the native. This is so when this house is as strong as, or stronger than, the fourth or tenth house, but if these latter houses are stronger they become more effective indicators than a relatively weakly aspected Ascendant.

Some astrologers, especially Charles A. Jayne, Jr., go by the axis; rather than referring to a conjunction of Saturn to the Descendant, for example, he states that there is an opposition of Saturn to the Ascendant, while, as a matter of fact, both these aspects occur and are relevant. The point made by Jayne is that the Ascendant is a more dominant element of the horizontal axis than is the Descendant. Applying this logic to the vertical axis, if either the Midheaven or the Nadir is more prominently aspected than is the horizontal axis, then the person concerned and his proneness to illness are more characteristic of the sign of the Midheaven and the planets in the fourth and tenth houses. Otherwise, the person concerned is more characteristic of the ascending sign and of the planets in the first and seventh houses. Squares by planets to either axis affect both angles of the axis, of course, but their effect on appearance, personality and proneness to disease is shown more on the Ascendant than on the Descendant, more on the Midheaven than on the Nadir.

Having relatively simplified this principle, it will be necessary to complicate it slightly.

8. *Use of the electrical axis, or Vertex and Anti-vertex angles, is essential to the adequate practice of astrology.*

The terms Vertex and Anti-vertex are unfortunate because they can be confused with the vertical axis (Midheaven and Nadir angles).

To clarify, an axis indicates two opposite angles, as follows:

Axis	*More Prominent Angle*	*Less Prominent Angle*
1. Horizontal	Ascendant	Descendant
2. Vertical	Midheaven	Nadir
3. Electrical	Vertex	Anti-vertex

The subject is further complicated because some writers apparently do not know the difference between an axis and an angle; they state that there are three angles in any chart when they mean that there are three axes, or six angles instead of the standard four.

The addition of the electrical axis to standard astrology is the only one I feel is essential. It was at first thought by its discoverers (Johndro and Jayne) to be indicative of meaningful contacts with unrelated second parties. I found it to be indicative of related second parties (4), as well. In the actual practice of astrology I have found that the vertex is substantially like the Ascendant, and the Anti-vertex is substantially like the Descendant, which gives two strings to the bow. The electrical axis itself is not my own discovery; I am strongly recommending this discovery by other people because it is so basically useful.

The Vertex is as simple to calculate, as is the Ascendant. Two pieces of information and a tables of houses are necessary.

The first piece of information is the co-latitude, which is obtained by subtracting the natal latitude from 90 degrees:

89 degrees	60 minutes	
- 42	22	= natal latitude
46 degrees	38 minutes	= co-latitude

The second piece of information is the location of the Nadir, which is used as a tenth house to find the Vertex. For example, natal Midheaven is 12 Leo 00; the Nadir is 12 Aquarius 00. Go to the tables of houses for the column marked 12 Aquarius for the Midheaven and find the corresponding Ascendant for the co-latitude. In this example, this is 12 Gemini and is the Vertex; the Anti-vertex is 12 Sagittarius, opposite.

Having outlined eight principles, I shall take an actual example of a patient who has diabetes mellitus, which is anatomically related to the sign Taurus, and consider it natally (see Diagram 1).

Pluto in Leo afflicts the horizontal and the vertical axes. Any sign in the quadrature could be diseased (principle 1), including Taurus. Because the affliction is angular, there is first degree proneness to fixed sign illness (principle 3).

Saturn, square the Moon and Venus, which are in turn opposition, all in common signs, indicates proneness to illness in this quadrature (principle 1) and is conjunction the vertex (principle 8); because Saturn is conjunction this angle, proneness to illness related to common signs is of the first degree (principle 3).

Venus, ruler of Taurus, is part of this afflicted T-square and hence is greatly afflicted (principle 2).

The Sun, conjunction Mars and Venus, is only relatively afflicted (principle 4), compared with the afflictions involving Pluto and Saturn, and is not relevant to the diabetes (principle 5). The Sun does not aspect any angle. Besides its affliction by

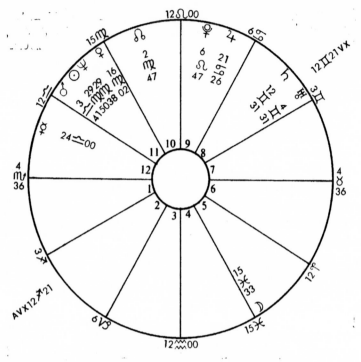

Diagram 1
Diabetic, September 23, 1942, 8:40 a.m., Boston

Mars and Neptune, the Sun is trine Uranus. The Moon is square
the electrical axis and is part of the T-square involving Saturn
and Venus, and is trine Jupiter.

There is no aspect between the Lights (principle 6).

Resistance to disease is active (Vertex in Gemini), but that in-
roads may be made by chronic disease is evident (Saturn closely
conjunction the Vertex). The *in mundo* conjunction of Pluto to
Saturn makes the resistance to disease, the bodily reaction to
chronic disease, tempestuous (principle 7); in this case collapse,
but no coma, recovery from the collapse but not without chronic
disease which was not successfully resisted—the diabetes

mellitus. Note in this chart that Uranus is quincunx the Ascendant and Mars quincunx the Descendant.

9. *The* in mundo *conjunction should not be omitted.*

The previous paragraph shows this to be so. *In mundo* conjunctions occur between planets conjunction any two of the three axes or conjunction both angles of one axis. The orb of conjunction of a planet to an angle is about two-thirds that of the interplanetary conjunction orb of eight degrees, or about five degrees maximum, as is the orb for a square to an angle. (Perhaps certain recent astrological authorities who delimit major aspect orbs to five degrees instead of the usual eight degrees have a confusion between interplanetary aspects and aspects of planets to angles. Many of these recent appearances over the horizon of astrology use so many words that 1 can't tell what they mean; maybe they don't know either.)

10. *The aspects that indicate afflictions within a given quadrature are necessarily the conjunction, square and opposition (because these are the only aspects which can interrelate planets and angles within a quadrature); the* in mundo *conjunction is included for this purpose only if the planets concerned are in the same quadrature and out of conjunction orb.*

In Diagram 1, although Pluto and Saturn are *in mundo* conjunction, they are in different quadratures and do not, for this reason, equate with a major planetary aspect within the same quadrature. This does not mean that both Pluto and Saturn do not intensify each other's affliction, but this is physiological.

11. *Other major aspects, which are adverse but in which the planets concerned are in different quadratures, or the planet and angle concerned are in different quadratures, are the quincunx, the parallel and the contraparallel; the latter two aspects with Pluto should be particularly noted because of this*

37

planet's aberrant declination.

Some astrologers use a wider orb, but I stick to one degree for the parallel and the contraparallel, and to two degrees for the quincunx. Between a planet and angle I use two-thirds this orb, 40 minutes for a parallel, 1 degree 20 minutes for the quincunx. I would not be at all surprised were the semisextile found to be of major intensity as an aspect when one or more of the planets concerned is a malefic; if so, the orb would probably not exceed two degrees. Perhaps Ptolemy's dilemma about inconjuncts (a term for both semisextile and quincunx) can be solved in that they cannot be applicable to principle 10, but can be applicable to principle 11. (*In mundo* conjunctions can be applicable to either principle.)

Other minor aspects are the semisquare and sesquiquadrate, more properly considered under the subject of midpoints in the next chapter.

12. *The gender of the planets should be considered—masculine Sun, Mars, Pluto; feminine Moon, Venus, Neptune; neuter Mercury, Saturn, Uranus. Jupiter is androgynous in that it is both masculine and feminine.*

Ruth Hale Oliver applies this classification to body types (4, 18) and uses it with her system of midpoints applied to physical-psychological types and their behavior. It is a bit more lucid than that described by deVore (10), wherein the Moon, Neptune and Venus are classified as feminine, and all other planets are classified as masculine (overweighted on the masculine side).

The musculo-skeletal system, geared for defense-offense, motion and the utilization of energy, is masculine; its general ruler is the Sun. This planet (and even more so Mars and Pluto), when afflicted, tends to active reaction against disease so that the reaction is inflammation, infection and sympathicotonia in which the thoracic viscera, the heart and lungs participate along with the musculo-skeletal system.

The viscerosensory system is geared for nurture, quiescence and parasympathetic reactivity. It is receptive, quietly parasympathicotonic when under stress. Its general ruler is the Moon; somatically and viscerally its sensation, and indeed bodily sensation in general, is governed by Venus. The only entirely feminine malefic planet, Neptune, when adversely aspected, produces very insidious reactions within the body; degenerations and tumors all too often are fully developed when symptoms finally appear. Contrast the immediate, violent reaction of afflicted Mars and, even more so of Pluto.

Jupiter augments either Neptune or the Moon. Jupiter also, as ruler of Sagittarius, has two sharply differentiated functions. Somatically masculine are the pelvis and thighs, which are under Sagittarius for the most part, as are their muscles. Viscerally feminine is the liver, under Sagittarius as well as Virgo, ruled by Jupiter and Mercury.

Androgynous Jupiter is strongly both masculine and feminine. Mercury is neither, since pure thought has attributes of neither sex. With Mercury as neuter are the malefics Saturn and Uranus (the antagonistic patricle and victim). Mercury generally rules and balances the phylogenetically more developed parts of the various systems. Saturn relates to flaccidity and stagnation of tone and reaction, Uranus relates to the opposite extremes of spasticity and overactivity. (This is why the parathyroid glands are under Aquarius, which is ruled by both the flaccid and the spastic neuter malefics; the parathyroids balance muscle tone.)

13. *Intermediate houses in medical astrology are related analogously to those in personality astrology.*

In certain connotations the first house may be read as analogous to Aries, the solar first house ruled by Mars. The second house may be read as Taurus, ruled by Venus; etc.

Traditionally, the sixth house relates to illness, and the twelfth to hospitalization (or the condition of being bedfast elsewhere); the eighth house to death, the manner of death, or near death; and the fourth to the end of the matter, which may mean the end of life, of illness or of both. I break with tradition somewhat on the latter house because the more the affliction to any or all angles, the more is the threat to life.

It also appears paradoxical that afflictions in the sixth and twelfth houses unaspected to angles denote only third-degree predilection to illness (principle 4) but yet also epitomize sickness and hospitalization traditionally.

Nonetheless, intermediate houses often fit into the delineation. This is especially so in cases wherein angles are not afflicted and there are no afflictions in angular houses.

I find that the use of wheels containing afflicted natal planets is more graphic than the usual chart. For example, the diabetic case shown in Diagram 1 is presented much more graphically in Diagram 2, which has the natal planets concerned inside the circle and the progressions outside. In this manner the astrologer looks only at what is relevant for the given time and event. In actual practice I do not precede the progressed planets with the letter "p," as shown, but rather put them outside the wheel in black ink; transits are put outside the wheel in red ink. This is much less complicated than the usual triple wheel which has all the natals in the inner wheel, all the progressions in the middle one and all the transits in the outer wheel.

14. Secondary progressions are sufficient for medical astrology. (This does not preclude primary directions, should these be the astrologer's best tool.)

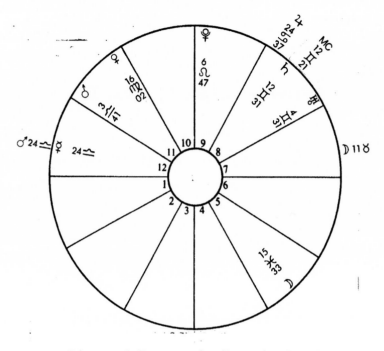

Diagram 2. Progressed to September 3, 1973

To be adequate, the astrologer must use all of them, progressing
the Midheaven according to the Sun's motion and calculating
the progressed Ascendant and Vertex accordingly.

Applicable progressions for early 1974, when the example case
(Diagram 2) developed diabetes, were:

a) pMC conjunction Saturn, Vertex
b) pJupiter square Mercury
c) pMars conjunction Mercury
d) pMoon, 11 Taurus, square Midheaven

Aspect a) signified decline in vitality and resistance because the
Vertex and interaspected T-square were affected, the Moon being square both Saturn and Vertex. Since Saturn was afflicted, it

in turn affected Pluto because of the *in mundo* conjunction; Saturn also affected Venus because of its square to this planet; both the fixed quadrature and the ruler of Taurus were afflicted. Aspects b) and c) denoted the collapse when the disease was first manifest; since Mercury is in the twelfth house, it indicates the hospitalization due to the collapse. Aspect d) pinpointed the locus of the illness, in the sign Taurus, and the time of onset.

15. Progressed stationary planets are very significant.

When a retrograde planet becomes stationary direct by progression, or a direct planet becomes stationary retrograde, there is a strong influence on the genethliacal chart. This is so a few days

(progressed years) before and after in the case of faster planets, or a week or more in the case of slower planets. (This information was told me by T. Patrick Davis and certainly works out.)

16. The return of a progressed planet to its natal place is very significant.

The same as principle 15, but more intense; imagine the equivalent of a Saturn return lasting several years, or the same with transaturnians (my own observation).

17. The slower the progressed planet, the more narrow its effective orb; the faster the planet, the wider the orb.

If I find progressed Saturn, for example, at 12 Taurus 15 and natal Pluto at 13 Leo 10, I forget it. But if I find progressed Saturn at 12 Taurus 45 and Pluto at 13 Leo 10, I consider the progression to be strong and likely to endure over a long period, analogous to principles 15 and 16. With fast planets, however, like Mercury and Venus, when they are moving a degree or more per progressed year, I take them two degrees applying and separating. It is a matter of proportion.

42

On the average, a progressed orb is about one-eighth that of a natal orb, but the proportionate variation is one-quarter to one-sixteenth. Orbs for some parallels can be very small, but they can be simultaneously very significant and prolonged in their effect.

Transits

18. Predilection to disease exists as a natal propensity. Progressions pinpoint the area where the propensity may become an actuality and, in time, the possible event. Transits bring the natal propensity, as activated by progressions, into actuality.

19. The slower the motion and the more prolonged the effect of transiting planets, especially when they are retrograde and repetitively aspect a natal planet exactly, the more powerful will be their effect. When two or more planets are so involved in adverse aspect and moving slowly, the prolonged cumulative effect is proportionately even more powerful.

20. Jupiter alone in adverse aspect may be sufficiently malefic to precipitate serious illness if its action is prolonged by retrogradation. In combination with malefics it will accentuate their effects.

21. Eclipses falling within eight degrees orb of a natal planet, or within five degrees orb of an angle, conjunction, square or opposition, are prone to precipitate illness, and their effects endure six or more months. Afflicted lunations have a like effect.

22. Event charts are essential when the time of birth is unknown, and are excellent supplements when the genethliacal chart is accurate.

The time when the illness occurs is used to erect an event chart. When the patient becomes sick abed, the event chart is known

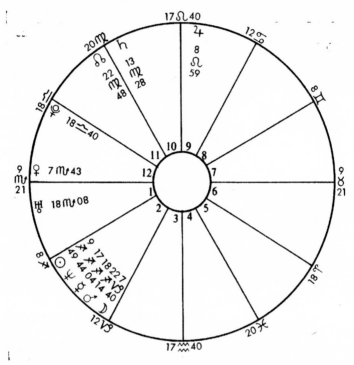

Diagram 3
Nosebleed, December 2, 1948, 4:22 a.m. EST, 71W00, 41N48

as a decumbiture chart; Barbara Watters gives examples of the latter in a case of diabetic coma and also an event chart of legal complications due to severe diabetic ketosis (29).

Diagram 3 is the chart of the onset of a severe nosebleed. The nasal mucous membrane is in Scorpio, in this chart clearly indicated by Venus, the Ascendant and Uranus in Scorpio. Venus and the Ascendant are afflicted by a close square from Jupiter in Leo, and Jupiter indicates expansion. There was such expansion that hospitalization was necessary, and it took three days before the bleeding entirely stopped. The sudden and unexpected onset of the bleeding is indicated by Uranus in Scorpio, closely conjunction the Midheaven, a first-degree affliction. The obvious cause of the bleeding was dry rhinitis, and Uranus typifies dryness.

There was also another illness, high blood pressure, previously unknown, which perhaps aggravated but did not cause the bleeding. Natal Mars is at 12 Aries, which is also the degree of the sixth house cusp of illness in the event chart, and afflicted Mars is one indication of hypertension especially when it is in a cardinal sign. Natal Mercury is at 19 Aries; transiting Pluto is closely opposition it and is in the twelfth house of hospitalization and hidden illness in the event chart.

Hospitalization did indeed occur shortly before midnight when the Moon was at 19 Capricorn square Pluto in the event chart and square Mercury in the natal. Mercury in the natal chart rules the twelfth house of hospitalization. The hospitalization ended when the bleeding was finally checked on December 5; transiting Moon had separated eight degrees from the Nadir of the event chart; the fourth house signified the end of the matter. Note the quincunxes of both luminaries; Sun to Descendant and Moon to Jupiter and the cusp of the eighth house, indicating that the condition was sufficiently critical to be dangerous. Had malefics been in like aspect, the condition would have been considerably more dangerous. As it was, the bleeding from the nose prevented possible stroke because it decreased the blood pressure.

IV

Additional Delineative Methods

DeLuce quite properly termed Indian astrology as constellational (8), as opposed to Western tropical astrology. Like many of us, he had the urge to grow, so he studied this entirely separate system, as did Sepharial earlier (26). Both found each system entirely workable. In medical astrology never will the twain meet; if, for example, 25 degrees of tropical Aries changes to constellational Pisces, there is a marked confusion between the feet and the head. This does not

mean that constellational medical astrology is unworkable, only that the system must be studied in context. This is an avenue of growth for the medical astrologer, one for which I have never had the time. One of the most interesting astrological interpretations that my wife and I have heard, however, was done by a Bangkok astrologer who used constellational astrology with some numerology. Unfortunately, because of a minor civil disturbance, we left Thailand without seeing him again.

Collectively, the Hamburg School of Astrology consists of the Ebertin system and Uranian astrology, and it may not be all baloney. I have had interpretations by both schools. The Uranian chart was remarkable in its art and workmanship and must have taken an enormous amount of time to complete. Many things are claimed by Uranian astrologers, but none, including their special planets, have been proven. Yet neither have they been disproved.

The Ebertin chart took a good deal of work also, and the reading was lucid. Ebertin has nearly everything written down and catalogued and even has a dictionary (11), which is not, as far as I can learn, in English. Epilepsy, for example is given as Sun at the midpoint of Uranus and Neptune. The trouble with the Ebertin system is that its details are given like pronouncements of Jehovah; the first degree of Virgo, for example, is the duodenum, and the intestine ends with the rectum in the seventh degree of Virgo. This conflicts with embryology, since the rectum, primitive urinary system and reproductive system all derive from the cloaca. The Ebertinian who showed me about the system stated it was derived as an ancillary aid to standard tropical astrology. This does not now appear to be the case according to a recent article which avers that the Ebertin system makes intermediate cusps unnecessary.

Nonetheless, I neither deride nor put down the Hamburg schools. I have the distinct feeling their good interpreters are good because of Ptolemy's "particular faculty," and would like to know if additional planets arc really "out there."

In my opinion, medical or any other astrology should be done by the standard tropical method if the astrologer is so trained. In practice, as differentiated from playing with another system for fun, the second system or systems should be used to recheck for accuracy. I do not believe systems should be mixed, but rather that each system should be used separately in terms of its own internal consistency, as did Sepharial and deLuce, and as did Firebrace in tropical and sidereal systems. (Sidereal is a constellational subvariant.) Should, of course, the tropical astrologer become more proficient in another system, such as constellational for example, then he could fall back on his tropical astrology when a recheck is necessary.

My own growth, expansion and search for new information has been within the relatively conservative framework of standard tropical astrology. I have experimented technologically with converse (secondary) progressions, degree attributes, fixed stars, solstice points, decanates and various kinds of progressed and transit charts. For a while I fiddled around with various primary directions and ended up agreeing with deLuce on the subject: "In conclusion therefore it can be assumed that equatorial arcs of direction are not to be relied upon to predict events in the life to time closer than six months. If more precise judgment is required in regard to time it must be obtained from some other method, such as transits, embolisms, horary questions, etc."(7). The same applies to secondaries, so it doesn't make much difference. Symbolic directions are controversial, but experimental, and I admire C.E.O. Carter's fortitude in initiating them. I would rather play with harmonic life point progressions, however.

Certain methods are of particular significance in rechecking and redefining medical astrological cases when they are not clear, and in reading finer nuances of the delineation. Continuing numerically from the previous chapter:

23. Stars are very significant in medical astrology.

Barbara Watters has culled out a couple of dozen stars she most frequently uses in mundane, horary and personality astrology (29). This information is the result of several decades of research and should not be taken lightly. Robson (24) is the best authority on the subject. He lists 110 stars with their exact positions as of January 1, 1920, and summarizes the opinions of various authorities about their action. The information is archaic but it is there. I use the conjunctions and oppositions of stars within a one degree orb (and am inclined to think that the square may be as valid). Since my orbs are small, I want to know where the star is located in a particular nativity with at least relative exactitude. Stars are not fixed; they move about 50.25 seconds annually, forward in longitude, or about a degree every three score years and ten (except Polaris, which is moving about 7.5 minutes annually, as are our magnetic poles, or a degree of longitude every decade). I have devised the following tables for use with Robson. Table 6 gives degrees, minutes and seconds to be added for each decade after 1920, or subtracted if before that year. Table 7 gives minutes and seconds to be added or subtracted for years one through nine as odd years more or less than even decades:

Example of use: Sharatan was at 2 Taurus 21 in 1920. To find its 1964 position, look for 1960 in the first column of Table 6; to the right of it is 0 33 38 to be added. For the remaining four

Table 6				Table 7		
Years	d	m	s	Years	s	m
1930-1910	0	08	22	1	0	50
1940-1900	0	16	44	2	1	40
1950-1890	0	25	16	3	2	31
1960-1880	0	33	38	4	3	21
1970-1870	0	41	00	5	4	11
1980-1860	0	50	22	6	5	02
1990-1850	0	58	44	7	5	52
2000-1840	1	07	06	8	6	42
2010-1830	1	18	28	9	7	32
2020-1820	1	26	50			

years, look on the left of Table 7 for the figure 4, and to the right of it is 3 21 to be added.

$$0\ 33\ 38$$
$$\underline{3\ 21}$$
$$0\ 36\ 59$$

Rounding this off, 0d 37m added to Sharatan's 1920 position, or 2 Taurus 58, is the star's position in 1964.

(This is enough accuracy for ordinary purposes. For more specific purposes Robson gives exact annual variations for each star. For example, Regulus moves 48.0 seconds annually. Using this calculation, the Aquarian Age will begin in 2016, whereas using 50.25 seconds it would begin in 2010, a figure I previously published (5), which is less accurate. Only in recent years has astronomical measurement equaled that of the Aztecs, who give an exact date and time in this decade for the New Age. We probably will have to wait until the 2010-2020 A.D. ephemeris comes out to confirm it, assuming we have not previously extinguished our species.)

24. Solstice points are significant natally, progressed, and transited.

My tables for determining solstice points in round numbers are in *Astropsychiatry* (4). I now calculate them by mental addition:

In fixed signs the first two, Taurus and Leo, are solstice, as are the latter two, Scorpio and Aquarius. Cardinal and mutable (common) signs interrelate. The second and last cardinal signs, Cancer and Capricorn, are solstice the signs previous to them, Gemini and Sagittarius, respectively. The first and third cardinal signs are adjacent to their opposites: Aries is solstice Virgo, the mutable sign next to Libra, which is opposition Aries; Libra is solstice Pisces, the mutable sign adjacent Aries, which is opposition Libra. Picture the natural zodiac or flat wheel with the west a mirror of the east for solstice points.

Once it is known which pairs are which, the degrees and minutes of planets and angles in each pair are added. If their sum is between 29 and 30 degrees, they are natally solstice within a degree.

If you want to know all natal solstice points, subtract all planets and angles from 30 degrees and put in the corresponding solstice sign. For example: Mars is at 20 Scorpio 15. Subtracted from 30 degrees, the longitude is 9d 34m. The sign Aquarius is solstice Scorpio, so 9 Aquarius 45 is exactly solstice Mars at 20 Scorpio 15. (Solstice points are, less precisely, also known as antiscions). A whole solstice chart could be erected if the astrologer so wished.

Both stars and solstice points are very interesting in the case of the diabetic discussed in the previous chapter. In fixed signs he had the following natal elements and solstices:

Natal	Solstice
Descendant 4 Taurus 36	23 Leo 24
Pluto 6 Leo 47	23 Taurus 13
Midheaven 12 Leo 00	18 Taurus 00
Ascendant 4 Scorpio 36	25 Aquarius 24
Nadir 12 Aquarius 00	18 Scorpio 00

Stars conjunction or opposition these points are Praesaepe, 6 Leo 26; North Asellus, 6 Leo 44 conjunction Pluto; Armus 11 Aquarius 56 conjunction the Nadir; and Capulus 23 Taurus 24, conjunction Pluto's solstice point.

At the time of the native's collapse transiting Mars had just passed Pluto's solstice point, and Jupiter had just passed the solstice point of the Ascendant, triggering the transits of these planets to the natal chart some six months before, when the illness apparently started. Mars had conjoined the Descendant, retrograding, and Jupiter had squared Pluto, also retrograding, in 1973.

Astrology may become more of a science in the future if it lives more literally up to its name, the study of the stars, which is aided by the study of solstice points, which in turn supply other data also not often noted.

25. Epochs are of epidemiological interest.

I have previously discussed epochs in terms of Jungian epochal astrology (5). To recapitulate the hypothesis briefly: Since the slower planets are the most powerful in their action, the cycles beginning with their grand mutation conjunctions endure until the conjunction occurs in the next sign. The slowest, and therefore the master, conjunction is that of Pluto and Neptune; the last time they conjoined was during the not-so-gay Nineties, a subcycle of their total Gemini epoch. At about this period the white plague, epidemic tuberculosis, occurred in northern Europe and America. Tuberculosis is a disease of Gemini. At the same time there was an enormous increase in mental illness, a primary thought disorder, Mercurial, Geminian. The number of state hospitals for the mentally ill and the number of tuberculosis sanitaria have multiplied several times since the nineties.

Today tuberculosis is still with us but there is not much of it; indeed, there is not as much as would be expected among our large populations of poorly housed and poorly fed people, and many sanitaria have outlived their usefulness. Like perennial paupers, the mentally ill are always with us, but there has been a change in their character; only one of the four traditional types of schizophrenia is at all common. Other types have appeared and, for better in some respects, for worse in others, our state hospitals are phasing out as rapidly as possible. The changes in both schizophrenia and tuberculosis began with the conjunction of Uranus and Pluto in Virgo, the sign of medical treatment. Towards the end of this century, Saturn, Uranus and Neptune will triply conjoin. Their epochal epidemiology should be interesting. Some pathologists believe that epidemiological changes are the result of subtle changes in the characteristics of the intracellular fluids, which are under Neptune.

26. Midpoint complexes are as important to function as zodiacal signs are to anatomy.

Technically, a midpoint is exactly half the distance between two planets (or other elements of the chart). A midpoint complex consists of a third planet (or other element of the chart) conjunction a midpoint. Really, there are always two midpoints concerned, exactly opposition, when a midpoint is noted. For example, if the Sun is at 2 Aries and the Moon at 2 Leo, their midpoint(s) are 2 Gemini and 2 Sagittarius, so there can be no opposition because a planet at either 2 Gemini or 2 Sagittarius is conjunction the midpoint.

The Oliver theory of midpoint complexes is well proven by her studies of suicide and homicide (both events are certainly total malfunctions) because her findings, her signatures, work in every case and are not applicable to non-suicidal or non-homicidal individuals, except that in the latter the signatures may show up in the victim's chart (4). According to her findings the planet that is midpoint the other two elements makes the complex operative if it is within eight degrees orb of the midpoint, the usual orb for a major aspect. When behavior pathology is concerned, a malefic is one of the planets of the two which form the midpoint, and the malefic is of a different gender (chapter III, principle 12). For example, Venus will be involved with Mars, a masculine planet, and with Saturn and Uranus, which are neuter. But Venus will not be involved with Neptune because the latter malefic, like Venus, is classified as feminine (see Diagram 4).

54

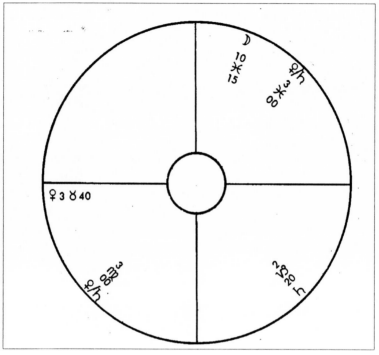

Diagram 4

The Moon at 10 Pisces 15 is 7 degrees 15 minutes from conjunction the midpoint of Venus and Saturn (Venus/Saturn). As written in astrological symbols, the equal sign is used to indicate the aspect: ☽ = ♀/♄ 3 ♍ ♓ 00.

It appears that the fastest moving planet of the two which form the midpoint is synchronous with the functional affliction. In Oliver's cases there was always a progression to either the midpoint, to one of the planets concerned or to the occupying planet or planets.

The reader might ask what this has to do with medical astrology. For one thing, the concept of the midpoint complex is not medically new. Raphael noted that a malefic equidistant from the Lights could be a natal sign of early death (23). Also, there might be equivalent events in the lives of the individual rather than active behavior, or equivalents of physical illness. Suicidal depression is a medical condition also. There are neurohorhormal imbalances, physiological disorders of function, which require medicinal correction by the psychiatrist in order that such deep depressions be relieved. Homicidal violence frequently is associated with temporal lobe syndrome, imbalance of the limbic system, and associated neurohormones which affect the amygdaloid nucleus, or apparently irremediable character disorders. Not only in astrology, but also in much of today's popular and technical literature, there is an unrealistic tendency to believe that major psychiatric illnesses and character disorders can be treated by the magic of interviews; major psychiatric illnesses are major concerns both as to their concomitant functional pathology and their treatment.

Such types of midpoints are applicable to many functional illnesses which are not psychoses—asthma, enteritis, colitis and a host of other conditions wherein there is no great amount of permanent structural change. For instance, in asthma, as well as searching the chart for afflictions in Gemini and/or other common signs, consider the midpoints of Mercury with non-neutral malefics—Mercury/Mars, Mercury/Neptune and Mercury/Pluto. The occupying planets are probably feminine—the Moon, Venus, Neptune and androgynous Jupiter—except in the case of Mercury/Neptune, in which Neptune is already feminine, because Mercury is the ruler of Gemini's function, and because the feminine planets indicate overbalance of the parasympathetic nervous system. (Asthma secondary to and resultant from decompensated heart disease is not true asthma, so the findings would be different.)

I have used the same delineation in studying schizophrenia psychiatrically, but as only one factor related to autonomic brain imbalance affecting the cerebral cortex, which is also in Gemini. This does not mean there is any direct relation between asthma and schizophrenia, but there is an analogical autonomic nervous system imbalance underlying both conditions as part of the astrological findings. This analogy is noted also in treatment, since schizophrenic medications derive from the antihistamines used to treat allergies. Astrology answers the question first propounded by Pottenger as to why there exists systemic, partial imbalance of the autonomic nervous system (20). For example, an extroverted, sthenic (mesomorphic) individual, with comparative overbalance of the sympathetic branch of the autonomic nervous system might have regional parasympathicotonia in a single organ or system, and as a consequence could develop an illness completely uncharacteristic of his general physical type. For example, a markedly sthenic individual will develop paranoid schizophrenia or pulmonary tuberculosis; neither illness is typical of this somatotype but may well show up in the patient's horoscope.

A fuller exposition of Oliver's hypothesis regarding male, female and neuter planets, which she calls by Sheldon's terms mesomorphic, endomorphic and ectomorphic, is in her *Physique, Temperament, and Psyche* (18). Epidemiology (principle 25) has changed in one respect since Sheldon published his hypothesis on schizophrenia; we rarely see three of the four classical types of schizophrenia. Only the paranoid type is seen commonly today, plus two newer types, undifferentiated and schizo-affective. (Psychiatric medications came into common use when Pluto went into Virgo, and one effect of its conjunction with Uranus in that sign in the sixties was the community mental health movement.) Oliver's monograph is well worth reading and re-reading, as is all of her work.

27. Principles of horary astrology may be applied to medical astrology.

Barbara Watters has a chapter on this (29). She notes, as do Carter (1) and Oliver (18), that the grand trine is not necessarily benefic. Ruth Oliver's explanation of this phenomenon tells us why this is so: a grand trine has three Oliver midpoint complexes. In electing surgical dates, Watters advises us to circumvent a void-of-course Moon or the Moon in the *via combusta*, invalid Ascendant, or Saturn conjunction the horizontal axis. She recommends that we avoid quincunxes by the heavy planets, especially to the Moon or Ascendant. She suggests bypassing planets in the degree of the Nodes, avoiding Mercury retrograde or the retrograde significator of the sign governing the part of the body concerned. She recommends selection of a time when a benefic is angular, and when aspects of the Moon during and immediately after the operation are favorable. To this I would add that the ruler of the sign concerned should not be peregrine.

Unless the surgeon is astrologically oriented and in control of the operating schedule (which are rare eventualities), the time of surgery will not be selected by the astrologer. (I have heard of only one exception—a neurosurgeon who scheduled an operation at 6:00 a.m., which meant he got the entire operating room staff in early and had to counter questions from various officials of the hospital as to why this irregularity had occurred.) About all the astrologer can do in actual practice is to suggest delay of elective surgery and to remember that most surgery is done in the morning. I have never read of it anywhere, but absolutely the worst time to have an operation is during the three days that precede the New Moon; like anything else attempted at this time, what is started is not likely to be completed. As far as surgery is concerned, this means that complications and sequellae requiring further surgery are more often than not likely to ensue and to continue indefinitely. If you suggest a delay, the Moon can pass into a more favorable sign, or an adverse aspect by a malefic may pass. I tend to try to delay elective surgery when

58

the transiting Moon is opposition or square planets in the zodiacal sign concerned with the anatomy involved, as well as when those planets are conjunction a transiting Moon that is afflicted. To suggest delay of emergency surgery is most inadvisable, since the consequence could be death; some nonelective (but not emergency) surgery can, however, be stalled a day or more.

28. Modern Arabic astrology is highly significant.

This is because, in terms of historical continuity, it goes back so far in time that its antiquity cannot be determined. Donatien Gravel of Montreal is going to write a book on Arabic astrology; he has been to North Africa and studied it. Gravel can tell where a person's scars are likely to be, and on which side of the body there will be more of them, whether he is left- or right-handed, whether his illnesses have been on the left or right side.

As to sides, he notes that planets in the first half of a sign relate to the left, and those in the latter half relate to the right, except in Gemini and Sagittarius, which are reversed. Those near the fifteenth degree are bilateral.

He and Henri Gazon, in the same city, use a combination of numerology with their tropical astrology, reminiscent of the numerology used by the constellational astrologer I met in Thailand. Gazon will not delineate without using stars, and I note that most of the star names are in Arabic, not the Alexandrian Greek of Ptolemy.

Chaldean decanates, Gravel states, are commonly used in Arabian astrology, and I note that Watters also advocates them. They are shown in Table 8.

Note that the first decan of Aries and the last decan of Pisces are each before and after the life point at 0 Aries and are both ruled by Mars; they are the only two consecutive decans ruled by the

Table 8. Chaldean Decanates

Sign	1st Decan	2nd Decan	3rd Decan
Aries, Scorpio	Mars	Sun	Venus
Taurus, Sagittarius	Mercury	Moon	Saturn
Gemini, Capricorn	Jupiter	Mars	Sun
Cancer, Aquarius	Venus	Mercury	Moon
Leo, Pisces	Saturn	Jupiter	Mars
Virgo	Sun	Venus	Mercury
Libra	Moon	Saturn	Jupiter

same planet. The signs opposition the life point, Virgo and Libra, have decan rulers particular only to their own signs.

Decans are calculated by the rulers of the days of the week beginning with Mars, ruler of Tuesday, as ruler of the first decan of Aries; Mercury, ruler of Wednesday, as ruler of the first decan of Taurus; Jupiter, ruler of Thursday, as ruler of the first decan of Gemini. Going down the table in this manner are also the planetary hours, which are approximately two hours each (each exactly one-sixth of the duration of the day and night respectively). To use the planetary hours, the second decan column is best. Begin at sunrise with the first planetary hour as the day ruler and continue consecutively. On Tuesday, for example, the first sixth of the day is ruled by Mars, the second by Mercury, etc.; the night likewise is divided into sixths.

Reading Table 8 horizontally, the ruler of each decan rules the day of the week two days previous to the ruler of the decan before it. For example. Mars, ruler of the first decan of Aries and Scorpio, rules Tuesday; the Sun, ruler of the second decan of these signs, rules Sunday, two days previous to Tuesday; Venus, ruler of their third decan, rules Friday, two days previous to Sunday; Mercury, ruler of the first decan of Taurus, rules Wednesday, two days previous to Friday; etc.

29. It is not necessarily an Arabic delineation, but I have found in case studies that the *septile aspect* (51 degrees 26 minutes) *may be the most stressful physically*. I picked the concept up from Oscar Webber, who states that the septile is psychologically the most compulsive. I think cusp planets and angles should, by Arabian theory, be as mesial or ambidextrous as planets or angles near the middle of the signs, but there is a difference when they are between signs. From 29 degrees of one sign to a degree in the next, or a few minutes more, is a potential area of congenital deformity or physical affliction, and it is frequently associated with septile aspects. This is hypothesis at this point, but the reader may find it an interesting one to explore if an unusual case occurs.

30. *Life point directions are interesting.*

I have twice mentioned the life point in this chapter, and also Carter's symbolic directions. Carter notes that his invention is a recovery, rather than a discovery, of "part of an Arcane system of inestimable antiquity and value" (2); "rediscovery" would be a more common word than "recovery," I. think. Carter directs planets by radix, one degree, a Naros fraction 20/35 to 21/35, duodenary or two-and-a-half degrees annually and in several other ways, per year of direction.

The idea of life point directions is even more unique because the planets are each considered as having different numerical values; consequently each planet has a different rate per directed year, added to and subtracted from 0 Aries. The converse is true as well, since regular directions are used. If we use the Sun at one degree annually, Mercury is half a degree, Venus one-third, the Moon a quarter, Mars a fifth, Jupiter a sixth, Saturn a seventh, Uranus an eighth, Neptune a ninth and Pluto a tenth of a degree (sec Table 9).

Table 9 was calculated using the Sun for a degree a year and

Table 9. Life Point Progressions (Sun, one degree a year)

Year	Mer	Ven	Moon	Mars	Jup	Sat	Uran	Nep	Plu
1	0:30	0:20	0:15	0:12	0:10	0:09	0:08	0:07	0:06
2	1:00	0:40	0:30	0:24	0:20	0:17	0:15	0:13	0:12
3	1:30	1:00	0:45	0:36	0:30	0:26	0:23	0:20	0:18
4	2:00	1:20	1:00	0:48	0:40	0:34	0:30	0:27	0:24
5	2:30	1:40	1:15	1:00	0:50	0:43	0:38	0:33	0:30
6	3:00	2:00	1:30	1:12	1:00	0:51	0:45	0:40	0:36
7	3:30	2:20	1:45	1:24	1:10	1:00	0:53	0:47	0:42
8	4:00	2:40	2:00	1:36	1:20	1:09	1:00	0:53	0:48
9	4:30	3:00	2:15	1:48	1:30	1:17	1:08	1:00	0:54
10	5:00	3:20	2:30	2:00	1:40	1:26	1:15	1:07	1:00
20	10:00	6:40	5:00	4:00	3:20	2:51	2:30	2:13	2:00
30	15:00	10:00	7:30	6:00	5:00	4:17	3:45	3:20	3:00
40	20:00	13:20	10:00	8:00	6:40	5:43	5:00	4:27	4:00
50	25:00	16:40	12:30	10:00	8:20	7:09	6:15	5:33	5:00
60	30:00	20:00	15:00	12:00	10:00	8:34	7:30	6:40	6:00
70	35:00	23:20	17:30	14:00	11:40	10:00	8:45	7:47	7:00
80	40:00	26:40	20:00	16:00	13:20	11:27	10:00	8:53	8:00

with the other planets in proportion. (Alternatively, Naibod's arc can be used, or the secondary progressed and converse progressed motions of the Sun and the planets taken in proportion. This requires more work but might be more accurate.) The planets are given in degrees and minutes. To use the progressions, add to and subtract from 0 Aries for the given year of life. For example, at 43 years of age, 43 degrees is added to and subtracted from 0 Aries for the Sun (17 Taurus and 13 Aquarius); for Mercury, from the table, 40 years (20 degrees) plus 3 years (1 degree 10 minutes) equals 21 degrees 30 minutes, which added and subtracted equals 21 Aries 30 and 8 Pisces 30. For Venus, 13 degrees 40 minutes plus 1 degree (14 degrees 40 minutes) is added and subtracted, which is 14 Aries 40 and 15 Pisces 20. And so forth through Pluto. These directions from the life point are aspected to the natal planets and angles. Note that Saturn does not progress out of the Arien Chaldean decans before and after the life point until the traditional age of three score and ten is reached, Uranus at 80 years of age, Neptune at 91 years, and Pluto at a century.

31. *Rectification..*

The rectification procedure is certainly advanced astrology, at least when it is done properly. It requires that the exact position of natal and progressed angles first be calculated in degrees and minutes from the time given.

Various astrologers have written about how to rectify by using primary directions; Charles Jayne wrote a small monograph about this method (16).

I use secondary progressions. Since the angles are to be corrected in rectification, obtain four major events relating to the angles. For the fourth and tenth houses I use relocations, death, illnesses, disgrace, business failure or anything else concerning the parents during childhood. "We moved during the summer of my third year about the time of my birthday." "My father went to jail about Easter when I was 8 years old." "My mother died in February 1948." I mean really major events; include relocations as such because they are psychologically very significant to the child—the whole world changes—and usually also to the parents, such as in occupational changes resulting in the move (change of employer is tenth house, although character of employment is sixth.)

Partnerships and their termination, not only marriage and divorce but also business partnerships and any kind of personal enmity, relate similarly to the descendant and the Anti-vertex. Remember that astrological marriage relates to date of the commitment, not of the civil ceremony, if any. Some astrologers state that in the case of second marriage the ninth house describes the partner; in the case of third marriages the eleventh house describes the partner; and so forth. This may well be; however, innate individual capacity for partnership is not variable, so for rectification purposes the Descendant and the Anti-vertex relate to any marriage.

In the case of severe illness, injury, or accident, an angle or angles of the chart will be involved, or the ruler of an angle, or both, if it is major, disastrous, life-threatening. When the human anatomy is properly correlated with the zodiac, much more major information for rectification purposes can be gathered, so medical astrology is a great aid for rectification. When the Vertex and the Anti-vertex are used, they also provide another string for the bow.

Having collected data on most tumultuous, significant and catastrophic events, the process of rectification begins. For each event, calculate exactly the progressed angles and planets for the birthday nearest to the event. Beginning with the earliest event, relate the relevant progressions to the natal chart, either angles progressed to natal significators, or planets progressed to natal angles; progressed planets to natal planets do not give information about angles. For the date of each event get the relevant progressions exactly (or as exactly as possible, since very often only the month of the event is remembered); this is done by proportion, and the difference is added to or subtracted from the planetary or angular progressed positions.

Next calculate how far away the progression is from exactitude for the given month or day; there will be progressions, half a degree or less, so many minutes plus or minus exact. There may not be many of them but they will be greatly significant, because only very significant events are used. Convert them into proportions of a whole degree. For example, Mercury is 20 minutes progressed separating (plus 20) from natal Sun, and its motion is 1 degree 30 minutes. Multiply the number of minutes from exact by 60, and divide by the motion in minutes, in this case 20 X 60 - 90 = 1.3 degrees. This is minus because Mercury is separating. If it were applying, the 1.3

degrees would be plus. The Ascendant, as well as the Vertex, Mercury, Mars and Venus, are converted in this manner; conversion of the Sun and Midheaven are not necessary as they are near enough. When everything is converted into proportions of 60 minutes, average it and subtract the figure from, or add the figure to, the natal Midheaven and adjust the angles accordingly (the Moon may require slight adjustment). Usually the figure obtained is minus, because recorded birth times are more likely to be one or several minutes after birth, since the time is taken after, not during, the action. Often the recorded times are correct or sufficiently correct that they do not need alteration.

Rectification should be tested. If two or three more significant events in the patient's life show the rectified Midheaven to be within a quarter or a third of a degree of accuracy, the rectification is sufficiently close; probably no chart can be rectified within less than 10 minutes on the Midheaven. I seldom do formal rectifications but, when doing them formally or informally, I usually inform the patient about an event, one which he did not tell me about. When this information is correct, as is usual, the rectification is very certain.

Good, experienced astrologers rectify informally whew they determine if a chart "works," meaning whether the progressions fall approximately exact at about the time the corresponding events occur.

Rectification "from scratch," when the time of birth is unknown, is more difficult. Several speculative charts must be erected and tested against several events until one is found that is quite exact. (A speculative chart verified by one or two events is not rectification, even if the astrologer is prestigious.) I find converse progressions very helpful in starting off the rectification, especially as they relate to the Midheaven and Nadir—parental events and/or moves in early childhood—as well as the usual secondary progressions. The process is considerably speeded up if early childhood events correlate with a given speculative chart, or if there is no correlation, the chart can be ruled out and discarded.

Speculative psychically derived times do not differ from other speculative times and charts. At least one astrologer considers them to be Divinely inspired. But, if so, the inventor of the better mousetrap was also so inspired. And psychic predictions which fail to manifest must either not be Divinely inspired, or they are the work of the Anti-christ (which I doubt). When on occasion I have determined an angle of a chart by means of my own telekinetic system, instead of considering the information to be Divine revelation, I have very thoroughly checked out the chart. The Lord helps them that help themselves. Very probably actual times could be obtained by autohypnotic or, better still, Silva Mind Control, programming of an astrologer; but they would still have to be proven. Silva Mind Control is particularly adapted to incrementing "that certain faculty" by which charts are interpreted, as well as being beneficial to the health and personality.

32. *The Vertex chart, or second natal chart, is as useful as the natal.*

There are four types of natal charts: 1) those with the horizon heavily aspected, 2) those with the electrical axis heavily aspected, 3) those with both these axes heavily aspected and 4) those with neither axis heavily aspected. When the Vertex/Anti-vertex is more heavily aspected, the Vertex chart is more graphic, and often the intermediate houses can be more pertinent. In the type of case in which both the horizontal and the electrical axes arc aspected quite heavily either chart may appertain. For example, in the case of the diabetic discussed in chapter III, the vertex was throw into prominence because the progressed Midheaven was square it and natal Saturn (Diagram 2). The Vertex chart shows Taurus-Scorpio across the sixth-twelfth house axis (Diagram 4a). They square the Midheaven and Nadir very closely. Note how graphic is the position of Saturn and Pluto, the *in mundo* conjunction planets. The progressed Moon is exactly on the twelfth house cusp; hospitalization is the twelfth cusp, and Taurus on that cusp is the sign associated with diabetes. The progressed Midheaven square Vertex and Saturn graphically show affliction to general health (first house).

To erect a Vertex chart, use the degree and sign of the natal fourth house as the tenth, in the tables of houses and put in the remainder of the cusps. Compare Diagram 4a with Diagram 1, Chapter III.

33. *The vertex should not be omitted when relocation is advised for medical reasons* (or for that matter any reason). Diagram 4a, with the afflicted Vertex on the horizon, is more graphic for this purpose than is Diagram 1. This Bostonian would be better off

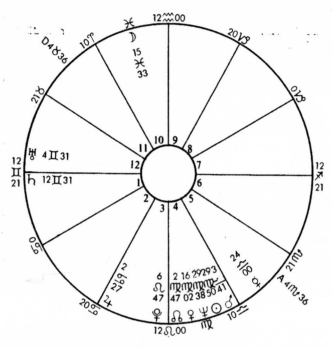

Diagram 4a
Vertex Chart of Diabetic

with Saturn well back into the twelfth or eleventh house, and
with Pluto back into the third or second house, removing the *in
mundo* conjunction and dissociating the T-square from angular
aspects. When advising relocation, remember that the co-latitude upon which the Vertex is based must be recalculated proportionately to the latitude. In some cases care must be taken
with both the horizontal and the electrical axes. (I calculate for
relocation in round numbers, and only calculate angles exactly
when a specific place is chosen.)

34. *Contraception and the Jonas method.*

About every 29½ days the Sun and Moon are the same distance
apart as they were at birth. On this and the three previous days,

conception is most likely to occur, and this can be prevented by sexual abstinence or contraception during the four days concerned. A second period of fertility is 15 days after the beginning of menstruation and three days before and after it; to be on the safe side, six days before and after the fifteenth day should be used. The four-day period is 70 to 85 percent fertile, the fifteenth day after menstruation and the three days before and after it are 15 to 30 percent fertile and the other mid-cycle days are two percent fertile. Ten days of abstinence or contraception, according to Jonas, are quite safe; safest are 16 days of abstinence or contraception. If the time of birth is not known, a day is added before and after each cycle. Jonas and colleagues found that in 1,250 cases the reliability of the method was 97.7 percent and they have so certified (19).

Not so authentic is Linda Goodman's notion that only five days abstinence per month is necessary (14). She is a lovely writer and her insights about Sun signs are the best I have ever read, but she bases her statements about the Jonas method on no authority, apparently, except an "exceptionally enlightening" telephone conversation with him using an interpreter, which "somewhat hampered" the conversation. Likely some of her readers will be exceptionally enlightened and somewhat hampered by pregnancy as a result. She also states that time of birth is necessary to use the Jonas method for infertility; it makes it easier but it is not necessary. Conception is most likely when the two monthly cycles overlap.

Astrological Birth Control is highly recommended for the reader who wants to know more about Jonas and associates (13). It is based on the literature and on personal interviews with Jonas and others by the authors. The source literature is not as yet, to my knowledge, available in English. Prevention of monstrosities, stillbirths and retardation, of which fewer cases were researched, are discussed in the book, and also predetermination of the baby's sex. Whether or not the astrologer uses the work of Jonas (personally I do), the book is well worth reading.

35. *Embolismic lunations are excellent supplements to progressions and transits, as are progressed monthly potentials.*

Embolismic lunation is the term used by Placidus for progressed charts erected for the time when the Sun and Moon are the same distance apart as they were at birth. He uses the first embolismic lunation after birth to represent a year of life, the second, two years of life, etc. as progressions generally and for health specifically. (Note that Jonas uses this same luminary arc as a transit in his work.) From these figures prognostications for the year, including health, are made. De Luce uses these lunations routinely as part of his *Complete Method of Prediction* (7), but it appears the method has fallen into disuse.

When I studied astrology I was taught to use the monthly potential, a chart erected for the time when the transiting Moon conjoins the natal Sun. I have adapted a progression of this figure to medical (and general) astrology by using each lunation after birth to equate with a year of life.

Both the figures have the advantage of expressing progressed relationships between the Sun and Moon in terms of a chart erected for the time of the event. The method for calculating them follows.

Progressed Embolismic Lunation

A. *Calculation of date of lunation.* It is much easier to calculate the date of lunation arithmetically than to thumb laboriously through the ephemeris. DeLuce describes one method of calculation (7); I think the following method is simpler.

Alan Leo was born August 7, 1860, and he died in his fifty-sev-

70

enth year. His natal Sun was at 14 Leo 53, and his natal Moon was at 15 Aries 22. The distance between the Sun and the Moon, measured counterclockwise, is 240 degrees 29 minutes of longitude. This is called the Moon's phase. The problem is to determine when this phase repeats 57 years after birth.

1. Multiply year of age by 0.0812
   Multiply fraction obtained by 12
   Multiply fraction obtained by 30

   57 X 0.0812 = 4.6284 years
   0.6284 X 12 = 7.5408 months
   0.5408 X 30 = 16 days

2. Add years, months and days to birthdate

Years	months	days
1860	8	7
+ 4	7	16
1865	3	23

3. The exact date of the lunation in the ephemeris is that, nearest to the date obtained.

On March 17,1865, the Sun is at 26 Pisces 56, and the Moon at 21 Scorpio 59, at noon; their phase is 234 degrees 57 minutes, and the natal phase will repeat on that date.

B. *Calculation of time of lunation.*

1. Subtract the 24-hour motion of the Sun from that of the Moon for the day of the lunation. This is the Moon's motion in excess of the Sun's.

Moon's motion	12d	15m
Sun's motion		- 1	00
Excess	11d	15m

2. Add Sun's longitude for the day of the lunation to the natal phase. If Sun is over 360 degrees, subtract this amount. Subtract Moon's longitude for the day of lunation. The Moon must overtake the Sun by this amount.

Sun 26 Pisces 56	356d	56m
Natal phase	+ 240	29
	597d	25
	- 360	
	237	25
Moon 21 Scorpio 59	- 231	59
Overtake	5d	26m

3. Divide overtake by excess (figure obtained in steps 1 and 2). The product is the time of the embolismic lunation at Greenwich. The permanent log is the difference between the logarithm for overtake and excess.

Log 5 26	0.6451	
- Log 11 15	- .3291	
permanent log	0.3160	
Antilog 0.3160	11h	36m

The antilog obtained is the time of the lunation at Greenwich. To obtain time for the cusps, subtract GMT if in Western Hemisphere, add GMT if in Eastern Hemisphere.

C. To recheck, calculate exact positions of the Sun and Moon; their phase should be the same as the natal phase.

Log Sun's motion	1.3802
Permanent Log	+ .3160
	1.6962

When using logs for this purpose, it is very simple to calculate the positions of Mercury, Venus, and Mars at the same time.

Antilog	0d	29m
Sun, March 17	+ 26 Pisces 56	
Sun's position	27 Pisces 25	

(Since both the Sun and Moon are moving significantly, the lunation may appear to be on a given day but is really on the preceding or following days; if the figures do not recheck, and the time of the lunation is close to 0 or 24 hours, try the day before or after as the case may be.)

Antilog	6d	55m
Moon, March 17	+ 21 Scorpio 59	
Moon's position	28 Scorpio 54	

Sun and Moon are 240 degrees 29 minutes apart.

Progressed Potential

To find the date, use exactly the same procedure as used to find the date of the embolismic lunation, except instead of multiplying the age by 0.0812 in the first step, multiply it by 0.075. Alan Leo's progressed potential occurred on November 19, 1864, when the transiting Moon was at 7 Leo 33.

The calculation of the exact time is similar to that of the embolismic lunation, since for purposes of calculation the Sun is considered to be stationary.

1. Subtract position of Moon in ephemeris from position of natal Sun. The remainder is the Moon's travel.

	14 Leo 03	
	- 7 Leo 33	
travel	6d	30 m

2. Determine 24-hour motion of the Moon from the ephemeris.

Motion   12d   07m

3.Divide travel by motion; the result will be the time the potential occurred at Greenwich

Log	6d 30m	0.5673
- Log	12d 07m	- .2986
(permanent log)		0.2705
Antilog	12h 52m	

Since Leo was born in London, the charts were erected for the time obtained. For people born elsewhere, add or subtract hours for the time zone concerned and calculate as any other chart.

No ACD is necessary for the embolism but one is necessary for the potential. Note that Leo's first potential occurred on August 15, eight days after he was born, on August 27 of a progressed year after birth or at 3.6 months of age, about November 25, 1860. Multiply the number of days after birth when the first lunation occurs by 0.45 to find the progressed age in months; in Leo's case 8 X 0.45 = 3.60. The second lunation after birth, in Leo's case September 12, 1860, corresponds with the progressed year beginning November 25, 1861.

The progressions can be progressed—yes, there are progressed progressions—at the rate of 12.4 days of life for each day after the progressed embolismic lunation occurs, or 13.2 days after the progressed potential occurs.

V

Cardinal Signs

Case 1: Alan Leo, Stroke

In a lecture delivered before the Astrological Lodge of London in memory of Alan Leo in 1965, the late C.E.O. Carter damned him with faint praise in several respects. Pertaining to Leo's astrology he noted that he was barred by the courts from direct forecasting as the result of violation of the fortune telling act, so consequently his conclusions "were recast in psychological terms."

"Actually," he said, "I do not think prediction so much appealed to Alan Leo. He used. a very simple method, the so-called progressed horoscope of Sepharial. This yielded the progressed angles and planets, and of course there were the transits. In my view a complete and satisfactory forecast cannot be made on these maps; indeed, I do not think his own progressed horoscope gave much evidence of his own end. . . . He did not use regressions . . . nor did he employ solar revolutionary maps, so far as I am aware."

Elsewhere in the article: "There was little conception of astrology and its vast implications. Mostly a matter of calculating primary directions [Carter must have meant secondary] and making predictions from these. The subject was pretty well a closed book for those not apt with figures." (1)

Carter noted the natal T-square and that Leo's chances of longevity were poor, mainly because natal Moon was square Mars, and said, "Certainly it was Moon in Aries added to Saturn on the Ascendant, which corresponds to Aries, that indicated the manner of his death, from cerebral apoplexy. . . . On the day of his death several planets were afflictive by transit, notably Saturn on Jupiter and Mars opposition to its own place. There is quite an array of one-degree directions, some very nearly exact:

- Uranus conjunction Jupiter lord eighth
- Mars conjunction eighth cusp (Placidus)
- Moon conjunction Uranus
- Uranus square Pluto
- Neptune square Ascendant (second out)."

Carter continued: "The only secondary progression appears to be Mercury square retrograde Mars. The progressed East Point was exactly opposed to the Moon."

In his *Encyclopedia of Astrology* (10) deVore points out that if either primary progressions or secondary directions are rejected as being astrologically invalid, then both would be invalid. If one cyclic synchronicity is denied, both must be rejected.

Checking Carter's directions with the natal chart reveals that the first two relate with the eighth house and therefore to Leo's death (Diagram 5).

Moon conjunction Uranus relates generally to sickness, because Uranus is the ruler of the sixth. Since Pluto is the natural ruler of Scorpio, the square of Uranus to Pluto may generally re-

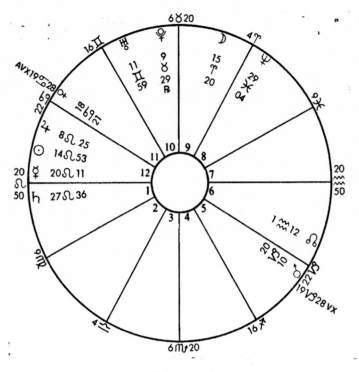

Diagram 5
Alan Leo, August 7, 1860, 5:49 a.m. GMT, London

late to the fourth house as the end of a matter, and it generally relates to death because Pluto is the zodiacal ruler of the eighth house. Neptune square Ascendant is all that relates to the natal delineation, and that aspect is two degrees out.

The actual adverse secondary progressions were as follows:

- Moon square Mercury applying three minutes
- Neptune quincunx Saturn separating nine minutes
- Mars conjunct North Node applying 22 minutes
- Mercury opposition Moon applying 12 minutes
- Sun quincunx Pluto separating 46 minutes

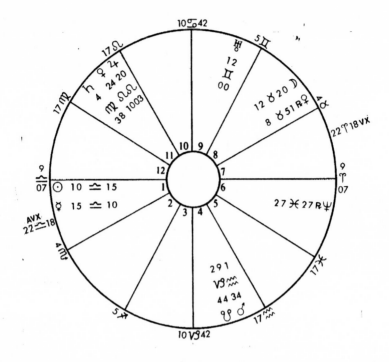

Diagram 6
Alan Leo, Progressed 1917

- Jupiter quincunx Mars applying seven minutes
- Jupiter conjunct Ascendant applying 47 minutes
- Jupiter quincunx Vertex separating 35 minutes
- Progressed Ascendant quincunx Pluto applying 22 minutes
- Progressed Vertex square Mars separating two degrees

The progressed chart (Diagram 6) shows the progressed Ascendant was not, as Carter said, exactly opposed to the Moon, so there must have been a typographical error, or he meant to say Mercury opposition Moon. That aspect would actuate the entire T-square, not only the Moon. Many astrologers do not use the quincunx aspect, and I think this is a mistake, especially in medical astrology in which the astrologer cannot afford as many mistakes as he can in personality or psychological astrology. There are no less than four progressed quincunxes.

The only basic technique I regularly use in addition to standard tropical astrology is the natal and progressed Vertex; and this is out of necessity, again to cut mistakes down to a human minimum. In Leo's natal chart, the Vertex at 19 Capricorn 28 is closely conjunction Mars, and Venus is closely conjunction the Anti-vertex; the Moon is square both. This intensifies the cardinal affliction from a minimal to a maximal proneness to illness, because the three planets concerned are in *in mundo* conjunction. (In fixed signs, Saturn, Mercury and Pluto are also *in mundo* conjunction, and also a very severe affliction. As related to hypertension, I would think first of cardiac hypertrophy as the most obvious explanation of this affliction, but this is something we will never know.) Using the Vertex in this case indicates a progressed quincunx which would not otherwise be delineated. Jupiter quincunx Vertex is delineated exactly as would be Jupiter quincunx Ascendant—expansion—and, due to the character of the aspect, the expansion is pathological. In this case Mars, the ruler of Aries, indicates expansion in an anatomical area of that sign and is consistent with apoplexy. Progressed Vertex square Mars indicates the condition probably began four years earlier when the progressed Vertex was conjunction the natal Moon.

Very often I use a few planets set up in a small wheel when doing progressions; and when there are many planets and the aspects are complex, I use two and even sometimes three wheels. I also, in my own work, put transits in red ink around the wheels. This would require costly color printing in this book, so I shall use progressions only around the wheels, and sometimes transiting lunations.

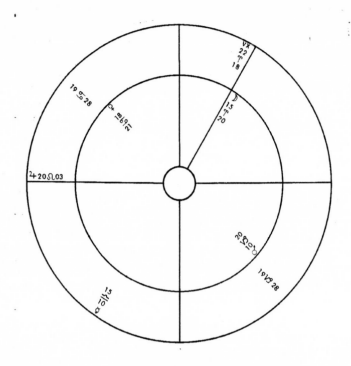

Diagram 7
Alan Leo, Cardinal Signs

In this case, Diagram 7 is of the natal cardinal planets and progressions to them. Diagram 8 is of the fixed signs. Note how in Diagram 7 progressed Mercury locks in the natal T-square and makes it a grand cross. This is augmented because the progressed Vertex-Anti-vertex axis is square the natal electrical axis. As noted, progressed Jupiter closely quincunx Mars indicates pathological expansion. Jupiter is also quincunx the Vertex, which indicates further augmentation of its aspect to Mars. In Diagram 8, Jupiter is again augmented in fixed signs because of its conjunction to the Ascendant; there are two quincunxes to Pluto and a third to Saturn. Either pattern, locked in T-square or multiple quincunxes as in these charts, or as in the yod aspect,

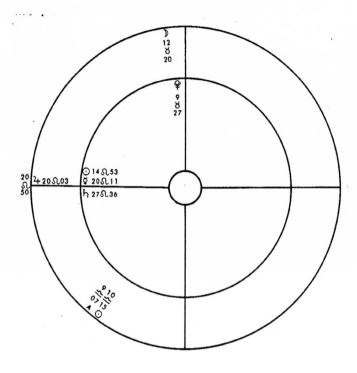

Diagram 8
Alan Leo, Fixed Signs

which has two quincunxes to the afflicted planets from planets sextile one another, is indicative of dangerous illness. There are more than enough secondary progressions to either cardinal or fixed signs to indicate a possible very serious medical condition or conditions, near death or actual death.

The transiting Moon went into Cancer, square Aries, shortly before 4:00 a.m. on the date of Leo's death. Often when only a few aspects show up by progression or, as in this case, transit, it is well to look to the parallels. There were no less than three transit contraparallels to natal Venus, part of the T-square, by the Sun, Mercury and Uranus. Neptune was parallel Jupiter, and Saturn was parallel the Sun. Also pertinent was a solar eclipse at 25 Cancer 51 on June 19, 1917, preceded by a lunar eclipse at 12 Capricorn 18, on July 4. The Full Moon of October 30, 1917, was at 6 Taurus 15, conjunction transiting Mercury and square transiting Mars and Neptune; the cusps were cardinal, and transiting Uranus was stationary direct semisextile Mars, applying by 12 minutes. This Moon almost exactly conjoined natal Midheaven. The two former eclipses, of course, augmented the cardinal T-square's natal and progressed afflictions. The third one, almost exactly conjunction the natal Midheaven, ticked off the fixed afflictions, both natal and progressed, which involved the natal *in mundo* conjunctions on fixed angles. In this case they also indicated dangerous illness.

By no means do I intend to derogate any method of primary directions; I chose this case as one in which secondaries are very obviously more relevant than the primary ones used. The good astrologer, proficient in basic technique, should not feel overwhelmed or feel derogated (as Carter derogated Leo) by techniques that are more complex than basic ones.

Speaking of more technical, supplementary techniques, the embolismic lunation, calculated in the previous chapter, is also significant.

Note that Pluto and Venus closely conjoin the Nadir of the chart. These, like the lunation preceding death, conjoin natal Midheaven and Pluto (Diagram 9).

Jupiter, in the twelfth embolismic house, closely opposition the conjunction of Uranus and Mars in the sixth epitomize expansion—explosion of the sickness and hospitalization axis—and are closely square natal Neptune in the house of death. Saturn in the embolismic chart is quincunx natal Neptune. In the progressed embolismic chart (Diagram 10) the Vertex in the eighth house is closely conjunction natal Ascendant, and the Gem-

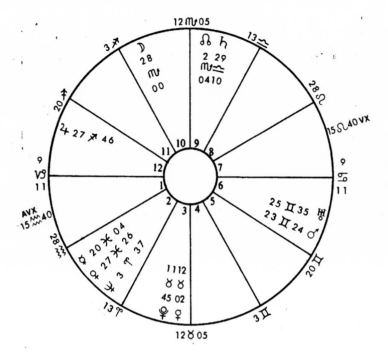

Diagram 9
Alan Leo, August 1, 1917, Progressed Embolismic Lunation

ini-Sagittarius opposition is closer to the sixth-twelfth house
cusps. Venus is almost exactly square the natal horizon, and the
North Node is almost exactly square the natal Nodes.

In all of these charts—natal, progressed, and embolismic—there is an emphasis on fixed signs as well as on cardinal
signs. Arteriosclerosis starts in the intima, the inner linings of
the arteries, in negative signs and then goes to the media, the
muscular part, in positive signs. In the head these signs are
Taurus and Aries, respectively. It is very possible that Leo had
cerebral arteriosclerosis with hypertension, making the apoplexy possible because of the underlying arterial weakness.

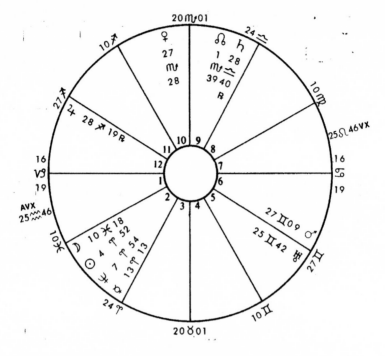

Diagram 10
Alan Leo, Chart 9 Progressed to November 1, 1917

Case 2: Esther

Her time of birth was not recorded, so I am using her solar chart; round numbers are sufficient (Diagram 11). I do not interpret solar charts by themselves, but when the time of illness is known, an event chart can be used in conjunction with the solar. Such charts are called decumbiture charts (3).

Were I to rectify this chart I would begin with the Ascendant in Scorpio because she was long-suffering, which would put the Moon in late Sagittarius, perhaps with the horizon in a square by Neptune. She had a rotten husband, whom she should have

84

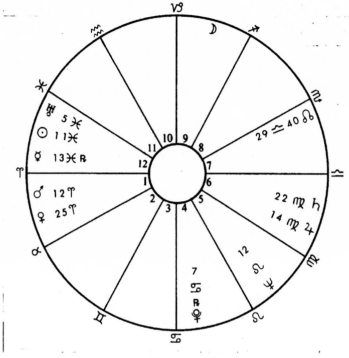

Diagram 11
Esther, Solar Chart, March 2, 1921

evicted years ago, a move which probably would have considerably prolonged her life.

Esther showed no signs of hypertension, nor did she have any
complaints that would make one suspect it. She certainly had no
arteriosclerosis and indeed looked younger than her chronolog-
ical age. She was, however, a heavy smoker, and the nicotine
could have produced some elevation of blood pressure.

Soon after she arose on May 21, 1978, she collapsed. When she
arrived at the hospital she was put into a respirator because she
had had a massive cerebral hemorrhage (Diagram 12). Her

85

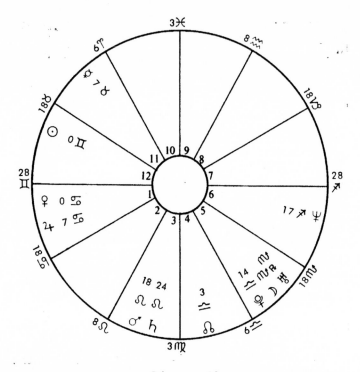

Diagram 12
Esther, Decumbiture, May 21, 1978, 6:00 a.m. EST,
Norton, Massachusetts

brain was dead. The plug was pulled three days later. I think she had an aneurism of an artery in the Circle of Willis (Aries) that ruptured. This is natally consistent with her cardinal T-square and the cardinal square in the decumbiture chart, which is intensified because Venus is conjunction the Ascendant. Note that transiting Jupiter, expansion, is conjunction natal Pluto.

Note the difference between the apoplexy, wherein both the intima (Taurus) and the media (Aries) of the arteries are involved, and the aneurism wherein the weakness is in the wall of the artery, Aries only.

86

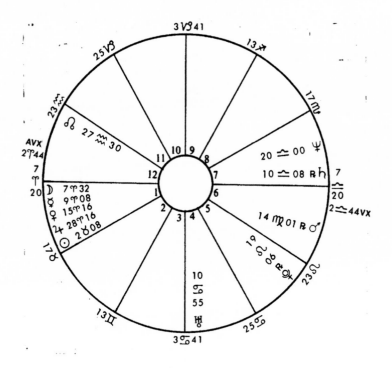

Diagram 13
Natal Chart, April 22, 1952, 4:14 a.m. EST,
Durham, New Hampshire

Case 3: Near Death Many Times

I do not have the date of this girl's first attack of rheumatic fever in childhood nor of her first near death but I have included the chart (Diagram 13) because of its remarkable afflictions—Moon, Mercury, Saturn, and Uranus in *in mundo* square; Venus and Jupiter opposition Neptune, and the inflammatory aspects Mars quincunx Venus, Moon contraparallel Pluto and Uranus parallel Pluto. The only planet not afflicted is the Sun, whose vitality with Jupiter is evidently what kept her alive. Consistent with rheumatic fever (when it affects the heart, it is under the sign of Cancer, because the lining, including the valves of the heart, are affected) is Uranus in Cancer afflicted by T-square; and the Moon, ruler of Cancer, which is afflicted and part of the T-square. The parallels to inflammatory-infectious-excoriative-ulcerative Pluto are also very important since they affect both a planet in, and the ruler of, Cancer. The progressions of the angles are obviously consistent with her contracting the disease very early in life. The first was Ascendant conjunction Moon, and the second was Nadir conjunction Uranus, nearby simultaneously with Descendant conjunction Saturn.

I have a case of rheumatic fever with as bad a chart as this one, but for reasons of confidentiality I cannot publish it. It has a grand cross, all planets are adversely aspected, and there is only one benefic aspect. When she came down with rheumatic fever in childhood, her parents moved down south. This saved her life; as the astrological result of the move was that her relocation changed the angles of her natal chart so they did not aspect malefics. She is now alive and active 30 years later, has no signs of heart trouble, and is outstanding in her professional field.

Case 4: Death by Astrological Misbelief

It is said that he who treats himself has a poor physician and a fool for a patient. The same applies to astrologers. This excellent amateur astrologer looked at his annual Ebertin graph in 1971 and did not think he would survive. In July he sustained a cardinal eclipse on his Ascendant, developed a fever and refused to go to a physician. The fever increased, and he took to his bed, refusing to go to a hospital. He died. He had thought he had cancer of the kidney, a diagnosis derived from his Ebertin interplanetary interrelationships as he interpreted them.

Neither his chart (Diagram 14) nor his symptoms pointed to

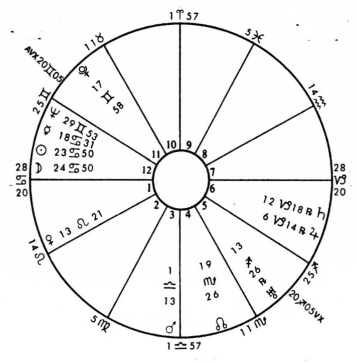

Diagram 14
July 16, 1901, 4:25 a.m. EST, 10E45, 51N50

anything but nephritis, consequent uremia, and death. He was strong and active, looked younger than his stated years, had an active mind, had no signs of arteriosclerosis and should have lived many more years.

He was a triple Cancerian. His natal luminaries were *in mundo* conjunction Mars and (using the Vertex) they were also conjunct Uranus and Pluto. Neptune was contraparallel both Saturn and Uranus, the latter two parallel in orb of one minute. This combination with both degenerative planets involved certainly makes one think of possible cancer, but neither Saturn nor Neptune is conjunction angles, so this possible proneness is not

89

maximal. During the conjunction of transiting Pluto and Uranus in the 1960s, he developed emphysema. He had moved out of the city smog to the country, stopped smoking and greatly improved to the point that he was no longer short of wind.

He had felt well, and in his semi-retirement had devoted himself to Ebertin astrology. This was the astrological correspondence of Pluto in Gemini opposition Uranus in Sagittarius and the three associated parallels.

Both the infectious planets, Pluto and Mars, were afflicted and on angles, and this was more consistent with the actual illness.

In higher animals there are two developmental shifts in the embryo affecting the kidney. As a consequence the glandular, vascular part of this organ is in the sign of Libra, whereas the hollow part and the capsule remain in Scorpio, the sign of the primitive cloaca. Consequently a sore throat (Taurus) will "go down" to the kidneys and cause pyelitis, pyelonephritis or cystitis in the opposite sign since it is also derived from the cloaca. Why this happens is a medical mystery, but not an astrological one, because both signs concerned are opposition in the fixed quadrature.

In this case, however, natal Mars is the most prominent planet in the partial cardinal T-square and, within less than a degree orb, is conjunction the Nadir. Libra represents the glandular part of the kidney, and Mars definitely represents infection. Pluto's *in mundo* conjunction indicates there can be severe, irreversible damage to tissue. The infection was sufficiently severe that it ruined the filtering apparatus of the kidney, so that the patient died of uremia. It took a week of high fever to destroy him (so I was later informed); an antibiotic definitely would have saved this man's life. The death was not sudden (despite the fact that the eighth house cusp is in Aquarius); he should have been to a physician a month before his illness. Progressions, when he

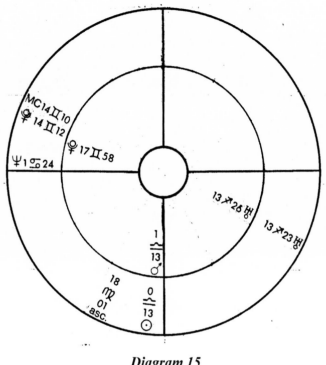

Diagram 15

died about the time of his birthday, were:

- Midheaven conjunction Anti-vertex
- Ascendant square Pluto
- Uranus conjunction Uranus
- Neptune square Mars, IC
- Sun conjunction Mars, IC

Note that the aspects in Diagram 15 are close. Two things were going on. The first was progressed Sun and Neptune afflicting Mars and progressed Ascendant square Pluto. This set off the infectious planets, Mars and Pluto, which are *in mundo* conjunction. The natal square between Mars and Jupiter augmented this conjunction. Secondly, the progression of Uranus almost exactly conjunction its own place not only stimulated the natal opposition in Gemini and Sagittarius, but also, because Uranus was so close to the Vertex, weakened the resistance. The same happened at the Anti-vertex, which was afflicted by the progression to Pluto and by the progressed Midheaven, which almost exactly conjoined it.

Note that the square of progressed Jupiter is within less than a degree orb to the natal sixth-twelfth house cusps at 5 Cancer. I am a little cautious about this axis, which has been much used by astrologers. Neither the natal nor the progressed sixth or twelfth house cusps in this chart gave more than general information. Nothing indicates the sign of the kidneys; only the quadrature is concerned. In Case 3 (Diagram 13), for example, the sixth house cusp is ruled by Leo, which indicates the heart in general but not the endocardium, under Cancer. I do not believe that the specifics of medical astrology appertain to these houses, although they were touted as such by Culpeper and deVillefranche in the 17th century (3, 9) and by Garrison in this decade (13). In this case the end of the matter (natal fourth house) was due to infection (natal Mars) of the vascular kidney (Libra), and the progressions were relevant to the primary natal affliction. Also in this case is progressed Uranus (which I consider a very powerful aspect), which returned to its natal place. This is indicative of possible death, since Uranus rules the eighth house. Despite the pretentions of some writers on the subject, my facts are derived from the examination of actual cases. The traditional houses are generally significant, but their significance is secondary, especially when the angular houses show maximal proneness to illness. They are not always significant in pinpointing the zodiacal correspondence with the anatomical area concerned, or in some cases not even the quadrature. Secondary, and indeed tertiary, delineations should be all means be taken into account; the matter is one of emphasis.

First, take the strongest, the most relevant, delineation and then modify it by indications of lesser force and intensity. In many cases the delineative emphasis of the sixth-twelfth houses is taken as primary, and the subsidiary delineation of the angles is taken as secondary. This throws matters out of proportion, because angular aspects of the planets are the stronger. The tail should not wag the dog.

By no means here or elsewhere within this book do I intend any derogation of Ebertinian astrology, which very likely works well within its own context, that of its own method. I have met on very friendly terms both Reinhold and Baldur Ebertin, and neither is the type of individual who tends to shove his ideas down another person's throat. Nor am I aware of any indication of death attributed to the Ebertin annual graph. The problem in all fields of preoccupation with "the new" and/or "the different" to the point of fanaticism and the exclusion of basic principles is a grave one. In this case it led literally to the grave. The Ebertin system is one good method to recheck basic medical astrology if one wants to take the time to do it.

Case 5: Arthritis

This patient (Diagram 16) has a marked natal affliction in fixed signs, a fixed T-square with Uranus conjunction the Midheaven and Mercury, and the Sun conjunction the Anti-vertex; Mercury is very closely square Mars. She has cardiac hypertrophy and arrhythmia. This latter is synchronous with the afflictions to Uranus, and while this planet is elevated because it is in its own sign, it is also in the sign of arrhythmia. The elevation means only that its influence is stronger. This influence is primarily due to the opposition of Mars, an explosive combination.

However, our concern is with arthritis and cardinal signs. She has had prepatellar bursitis (water on the knee) on the right knee

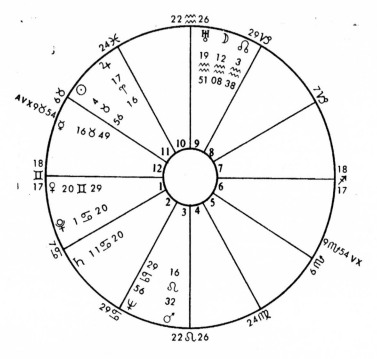

Diagram 16
Arthritis, April 25, 1916, 7:10 a.m. EST, Boston

and also arthritis since 1975. The knee joint and its associated bursa are in Capricorn, so the cardinal quadrature is involved. There is also an associated arthritis of the right shoulder with severe limitation of motion. The sign concerned is Cancer, also cardinal, because although the shoulder girdle and upper extremities are in the positive sign Gemini, their joints are in the negative sign of Cancer.

The only natal planets in aspect in cardinal signs (Diagram 17) are Jupiter and Saturn, which are square. However, Neptune is just barely in Cancer and is square the Sun. Pluto is in Cancer but not aspected to other cardinals, unless its semisextile to

94

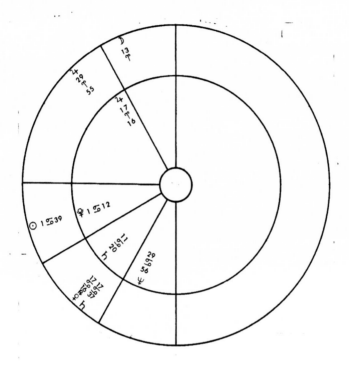

Diagram 17

Neptune is taken. I am prone to take it because both planets concerned are malefic. Pluto is inflammatory, Neptune is degenerative and Saturn is concretizing; Jupiter intensifies the reaction.
Every cardinal natal planet was activated by progression in
1975. On the patient's birthday and subsequently there was a
transiting cardinal T-square comprising Saturn, Jupiter and
Pluto. Saturn conjunction and Uranus square transited natal
Neptune by August, and Jupiter was square Neptune in 1976.
This is consistent with a right-sided affliction, severe and irreversible.

VI

Fixed and Mutable Signs

This natal chart (Diagram 18) is typical of a strong predisposition to diseases in zodiacal areas corresponding with the fixed signs.

Where the heart is concerned the Leo-Aquarius axis is anatomically involved, Leo being the heart muscle and the anatomical site of infarction due to coronary thrombosis. Aquarius is anatomically associated with cardiac arrhythmia and fibrillation. In this case Saturn in Aquarius is conjunction the Anti-vertex and the South Node. The Sun, ruler of Leo, in turn is conjunction the Midheaven. They are in *in mundo* conjunction, and the Sun additionally is closely square the Vertex. The Sun is opposition Algol, intensifying the predilection to illness. That illness would be sudden and unexpected is shown by the fact that Uranus is also *in mundo* conjunction the other two planets because of its conjunction to the Ascendant.

At the time of his death, March 5, 1966 (Diagram 19), progressed North Node was at 22 Leo 16, separating nine minutes from the natal Vertex. Progressed Jupiter at 26 Taurus 29, retro-

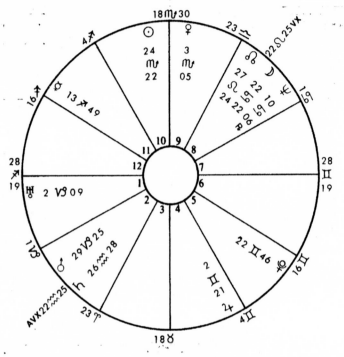

Diagram 18
Mischa Auer, November 17, 1905, 11:17 LMT, Leningrad

grading very slowly and only four days prior to its stationary position, was closely square Saturn. The progressed Vertex was applying within a degree to a conjunction to the Midheaven. Progressed Mercury was separating three degrees past its conjunction to Uranus, indicating the prior beginning of the disease, or the tendency to it. There had been a solar eclipse the November preceding death, which was conjunction transiting Neptune; it was conjunction natal Midheaven and Sun, square natal Vertex and Saturn.

At the time of death, transiting Neptune, retrograde, was separating 17 minutes from a square to the natal Vertex; the Full

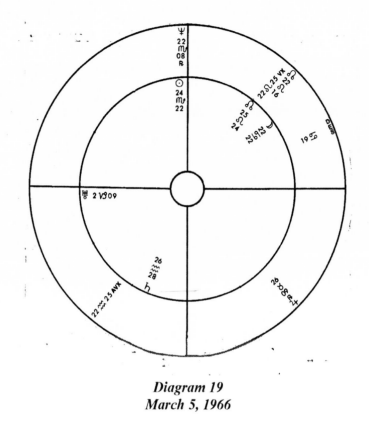

Diagram 19
March 5, 1966

Moon conjunction Uranus was square the natal sixth-twelfth house axis and Mercury. Natal Mercury was conjunction the cusp of the twelfth house, ruled the sixth, and was in mutual reception with Jupiter. There, were no adverse transits to the eighth house, but the progressed Nadir was closely conjunction its cusp.

Case 7: Lyndon Johnson, Heart Disease

I would not, myself, take LBJ's Jupiter as quite conjunction his Ascendant, even using a wide orb. (Were it to be taken as a con-

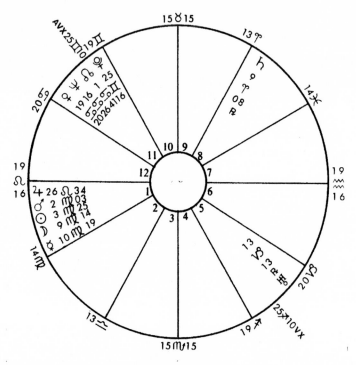

Diagram 20
Lyndon B. Johnson, August 27, 1908, 4:29 a.m. LMT,
Stonewall, Texas

junction, it would then be *in mundo* conjunction Pluto, which is conjunction the Anti-vertex.) Jupiter is, however, afflicted, because it is conjunction Mars. The affliction is augmented by the conjunction of both Jupiter and Mars to the Sun. There is a moderate proneness to illness in fixed signs.

General proneness to illness in cardinal signs as related to houses and angles is minimal, because none of them are conjunction natal angles. But, since no less than three malefics are involved in the T-square in this particular case, the proneness is certainly moderate. The combination of Saturn and Neptune is

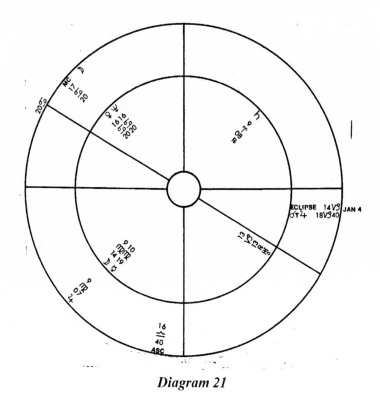

Diagram 21

degenerative as a rule; Johnson aged greatly in office. He probably was arteriosclerotic; with Neptune in Cancer in this case I think of arteriosclerotic heart disease as related to that same sign (of course Neptune in Cancer could mean many other things) as a more or less normal manifestation of aging. Johnson probably had a personal interest in campaigning against heart disease and stroke; he died of the former January 11, 1973.

Progressions at the time of his death indicate there were no effective fixed sign planetary progressions (Diagram 21). Progressed Moon was conjunction natal Neptune, and progressed Ascendant was square this planet. Progressed Jupiter, within only two minutes of exact orb, was conjunction the Moon, ruler of Cancer (not the Sun, ruler of Leo). Progressed Midheaven was conjunction Venus. Here are three progressions affecting the sign of Cancer, and a fourth one affecting its ruler. The linings of the heart and aortic arch are in Cancer, and this is consistent with arteriosclerotic heart disease. Progressed Vertex square natal Jupiter is consistent with heart disease in fixed signs, but only as a final coronary attack, the result of pathology in anatomical areas in Cancer.

Comparing Case 3, there is also an affliction in cardinal signs and related rheumatic cardiac disease of the valves, which are in Cancer. In LBJ's case there is a different condition, aging, but the sign of Cancer was also involved degeneratively rather than infectiously, the heart failing to function because it simply wore out. In Mischa Auer's case there was a direct impairment of the cardiac muscle under Leo, and the progressions are plain in fixed signs.

Confirming Johnson again are the transits, a cardinal Full Moon four days prior to death, with Mercury, Venus, Uranus and Pluto all in cardinal signs, and the remaining planets in common signs. There were no planets in fixed signs.

It is obvious there are several types of delineation that are consistent with several types of heart disease.

Case 8: Eisenhower

Eisenhower had natally what I call the kite configuration (Diagram 22), a grand trine plus a fourth planet that opposes one planet, forms the trine, and sextiles the other two. It is a "locked in" natal configuration, more synchronized than an uncomplicated grand trine. In Eisenhower's case the grand trine was in air with Venus opposing the Gemini planets and sextile Jupiter and Mercury in the other two air signs. He also had a T-square

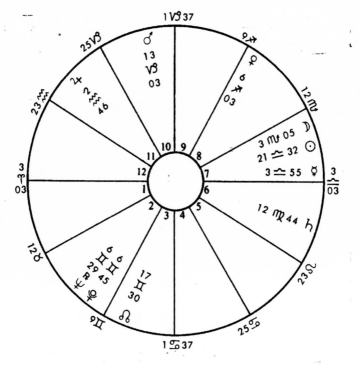

Diagram 22
Eisenhower, October 14, 1890, 5:00 p.m., Denison, Texas

in common signs and a close square between the Moon and Jupiter in fixed signs. Neither of these latter afflictions was conjunction angles nor in angular houses, so the proneness to associated illness is minimal. This does not mean it is non-existent. In this case they worked together when he had his first heart attack September 24, 1955.

No 64-year-old, and indeed no man 25 years younger, should go from sea level to an altitude of 6,000 feet and indulge in more than minimal physical activity. The air is rare at high altitudes, and there is a relative air hunger until the body adapts by manufacturing a higher percentage of hemoglobin and a greater number of red blood cells. At 6,000 feet this adjustment takes a few weeks. Until one adapts to the altitude, the exertion of normal walking can produce a shortness of breath. It is easy to fall asleep in a chair in the daytime, and the heart action is often accelerated. Since the heart is undergoing more strain, the body is consequently more susceptible to heart disease.

The most prominent planets in Eisenhower's natal T-square are in Gemini. At the time of his first heart attack, his progressed Midheaven at 5 Pisces 14 was applying square these planets and Venus, which in this particular case is indicative of possible functional impairment. The natal Sun, ruler of Leo (the heart muscle), was squared by progressed Moon at 23 Cancer. Natal Uranus, conjunction the natal Sun, and the ruler of Aquarius (the complex innervation of the heart) is opposed by progressed Mercury at 27 Capricorn 23. Because of their conjunction, what affects one of those conjoined planets would affect the other one. Two ephemeris days after this progressed year Saturn was stationary direct, which affects progressed year 1955. Progressed Pluto in 1955 (Diagram 23) was at 7 Gemini 34, retrograde, just six minutes separating from the natal planet, still in orb and highly significant. So there were multiple significant progressions to both cardinal and mutable planets, including the ruler of the signs of the heart and of its neurological innervation. The progressed stage was set for the transiting planets—among them the bad actors.

On the day of the attack transiting Neptune was at 26 Libra 59, having exactly conjoined natal Uranus on the previous September 16, on which date there was a Full Moon. Ike's attack was on the day of the next Quarter Moon, when the Sun and Moon were within the first degree of Libra and Capricorn, respectively, affecting all the natal angles. Transiting Uranus was at 1 Leo 26 opposition natal Jupiter, so the natal fixed sign square also was affected.

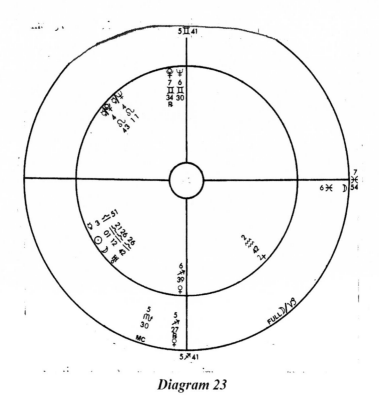

Diagram 23

Ike was a rugged guy and lived two more decades; his is a good chart to compare with Mischa Auer's. With the collaboration of a pathologist, the astrology of people who have advanced arteriosclerosis in their 60's, and occasionally even earlier, could be compared with those people who are not really old until their 80's.

Case 9: Multiple Illnesses

If you follow the major illnesses of people over several decades, you find they very often shift and change. Or if the illness is chronic and irremediable, the complications and sequellae shift and change. Sometimes illnesses are confined to a single affliction, like diabetes mellitus and its complications. In other cases different quadratures are coincident with different diseases at different times in an individual lifetime. In still other cases a single sign in a natal chart is synchronous with different diseases which, at different times, relate primarily to two or more signs of the quadrature.

In LBJ's and Ike's cases a solitary planet in a fixed sign was not especially relevant, if relevant at all, to the causes of their heart disease, except that it was Jupiter. Perhaps this served to prevent them from dying earlier than they did.

In Case 9 (Diagram 24) the Sun and the Moon are in a fixed sign, Taurus, and the patient's major illnesses relate primarily to this and to two other fixed signs. Her natal Sun was closely conjunction the Anti-vertex, and the Vertex and Anti-vertex were conjunction the sixth and twelfth houses. Her Moon was in the twelfth house and was square the Midheaven. Apparently more afflicting was a massive opposition in Gemini-Sagittarius, but in this woman's chart it related primarily to events in her life. This was analogous to Eisenhower's affliction in mutable signs; he compensated by leadership even after his attack on the golf course. The social history is as important in medical astrology as it is in regular medical practice. Indeed I think it is more important because situations, physical and emotional illnesses interweave and interrelate synchronous with progressions and transits. Often a situation will be by-passed, and physical illness will ensue as an equivalent. Or both the situation and the physical condition will be by-passed and emotional cases will become prominent. Medical astrology does not differ from other types of astrology in that multiple stresses synchronous with aspects at a given time are defined in terms of their existence in various spheres. The astrologer's function is to determine the best means of handling the stress.

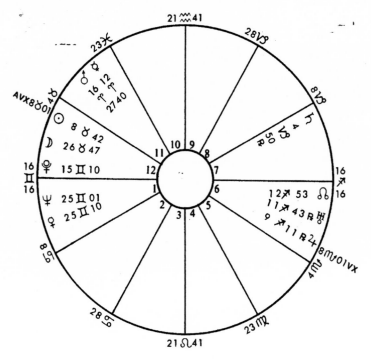

Diagram 24
Case 9, April 29, 1900, 7:00 a.m. EST, New York City

At 25 years of age this patient had hyperthyroidism (overactive thyroid). The gland is in Taurus. Progressed Sun (in Diagram 25) was applying conjunction her natal Moon, and the progressed Anti-vertex also conjoined the Moon exactly about the time of her birthday. Transiting Saturn, which had been retrograding, was conjunction the natal Vertex and opposition natal Sun; Neptune had been retrograding conjunction the natal Nadir. In 1925, there were three eclipses in fixed signs, none of them in Taurus.

In 1940 (Diagram 26) she had coronary disease. She was 79-years-old when I last heard of her, so I assume this must

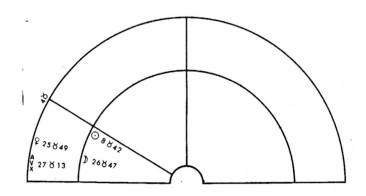

Diagram 25

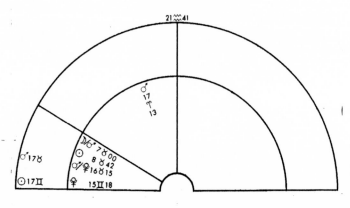

Diagram 26

have been functional for her to live so long. There are two mid-points that relate to the natal Sun, ruler of Leo. One is Moon/Mars at 7 Taurus/Scorpio 00, and the other is Mars/Pluto at 16 Taurus/Scorpio 15. Progressed Mars conjoined the latter in 1940, and progressed Sun was conjunction the Ascendant and Pluto.

During this year transiting Uranus, retrograding, was square the Midheaven and conjunction Mars/Pluto. Transiting Saturn con-

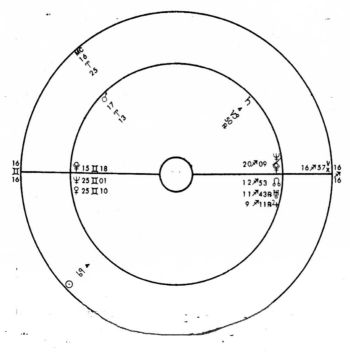

Diagram 27

joined the natal Sun, Anti-vertex, twelfth house cusp and
Moon/Mars. Nearly everything involved was in Taurus or on
the Taurus/Scorpio axis. However, the Sun, ruler of Leo, was
involved functionally as shown by the progression to
Mars/Pluto, to which it forms a conjunction, and by the transit
conjunction of Saturn.

In 1957 (Diagram 27) the patient contracted glaucoma, again a
functional disease. The patient had had illnesses involving
Taurus and Leo; now Aquarius was involved. (While the eye-
ball is generally under Aries, except for the sensory retina in
Taurus, the clear fluid is under Aquarius, so that glaucoma is an
Arian-Aquarian illness.) Progressed Midheaven was applying

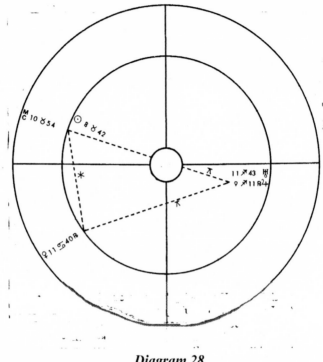

Diagram 28

conjunction natal Mars, ruler of Aries, in its own sign, and progressed Vertex was conjunction the Ascendant. Here the very
complex Gemini/Sagittarius opposition, because it includes
Uranus, ruler of Aquarius, comes into the patient's illness. Uranus, the lunar Nodes, and the horizon are all conjunction Neptune. Pluto at 20 Gemini/Sagittarius 09; by association Jupiter
and Venus are also involved. The conjunction of this progressed
Vertex to the Descendant is the culmination of blanketing progressions which successively affected Jupiter, Uranus, the
Nodes and Pluto. It is also square the Midheaven in Aquarius.
Progressed Sun was opposition Saturn, one of the rulers of this
sign. In 1957, Saturn, retrograding, conjoined Uranus, the other
ruler of Aquarius, and it was squared by transiting Uranus.

As she grew older the patient had arteriosclerotic heart disease, there having been repetition other coronary attack of 1940. Because her heart was wearing out, she was on digitalis, getting along uneventfully. Suddenly on May 2, 1978 (Diagram 28), three days after her seventy-eighth birthday, she suffered cardiac arrest and very nearly died.

Her progressed Midheaven was at 10 Taurus 54 at that time, conjunction the twelfth house cusp and quincunx Uranus. This quincunx reinforced the natal quincunxes of Sun to Uranus and Jupiter (the progressed Ascendant was conjunction the Nadir, but two degrees applying), and Venus was also quincunx these planets, just three degrees separating from exact aspect. This was the familiar yod aspect, a locked-in configuration. I thought she would survive because the progressed Ascendant was not close enough to the natal Nadir to be effective, for one thing.

On the day of the attack, progressed Sun reinforced the natal progressed quincunxes to Uranus from Taurus, and Neptune was conjunction the Descendant.

Transiting Pluto was opposition natal Mercury, and transiting Uranus was quincunx this planet. The affliction of Aries was consistent with cerebral thrombosis. Her mind was not right after the attack, consistent with Mercury's rule of the intellectual function.

Case 10: Double Taurus, Colitis

In the previous case all signs but Scorpio were diseased in the anatomical area of the fixed signs throughout the patient's lifetime. The patient in Case 10 had colitis (Scorpio). Both her lights in Taurus are square Mars and Pluto, the inflammatory planets, in Leo. The colitis began when she was 10-years-old and recovered spontaneously when she was 30, at which time

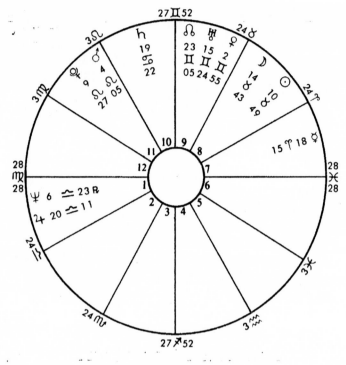

Diagram 29
Case 10, May 1, 1946, 3:00 p.m. EST,
Claremont, New Hampshire

she lost a lot of weight, having previously been obese. Colitis is consistent with the luminaries in the eighth solar house of Scorpio, square both the rulers of this sign.

Case 11: Vivian Leigh, Tuberculosis

Vivian Leigh (Diagram 30) contracted tuberculosis in 1945, and it was diagnosed about July 15 of that year. She had never taken good care of herself, smoking and drinking too much. Mercury, ruler of Gemini, was in the opposite sign, Sagittarius,

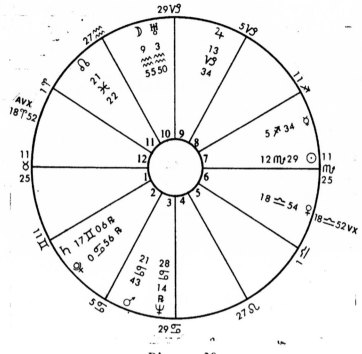

Diagram 30
Vivian Leigh, November 5, 1913, Darjeeling, India

opposition Saturn in Gemini by sign only. Neither Mercury nor
Saturn was adversely aspected to angles or in angular houses;
there appears to be little natal predilection to diseases in mutable signs until the parallels are examined. Neptune is parallel
Saturn, and Mercury is parallel Jupiter and contraparallel Mars,
so the predilection to diseases in common signs is quite strong.

There were no progressed parallels in orb to these natal positions in 1946. The progressed Sun was two degrees applying to
opposition Saturn, and there were no other progressions close
enough to be significant.

"... on a grim February day," says her biographer (12), "Notley Abbey stood grim and forbidding in the chill winter cold." Despite "burst pipes, the lack of heat . . . the total absence of modern kitchen and bathroom facilities . . .", the Oliviers looked at Notley Abbey, and soon. bought it. Nothing could be more environmentally conducive to precipitating tuberculosis in an emotionally labile, hard-driving woman who smoked and drank too much. The illness was clearly avoidable, which is consistent with the single progression.

On May 20, transiting Pluto was contraparallel natal Mercury; Saturn was quincunx Mercury August 4, 1944, January 20 and April 19, 1945. When the illness was diagnosed in July, transiting Uranus was applying to a conjunction to natal Saturn. She recovered sufficiently to accompany her family to New York in May 1946; the last transit conjunction of Uranus to Saturn was on June 1, 1946. What was apparently minimal tuberculosis went into remission. It was probably in the right lung. On June 10, 1945, there was a New Moon at 18 Gemini 55 conjunction transiting Uranus at 13 Gemini 35 and Mercury at 13 Gemini 33; it was square Jupiter at 18 Virgo 36. This major affliction to natal Saturn probably triggered the illness from incubation period to actual disease. Jupiter's first square to Saturn was the previous October, when the fall was unseasonably cold.

She died sometime between 10:30 and 10:45 a.m., July 7, 1967, of advanced bilateral tuberculosis at "Tickerage Mill . . . about 45 miles from London, a short distance from a lovely old village. . . ." (12). Leigh's biographer does not tell us which old village. Progressed Ascendant was at 6 Cancer 16, quincunx Mercury. Progressed Moon was at 26 Capricorn opposition Neptune—natally parallel Saturn—and applying conjunct the Midheaven. The semisextile of progressed Mars at 17 Cancer 14 retrograde applying closely to Saturn was also significant.

The New Moon at 14 Cancer 53 conjunction transiting Mercury

and square Mars and Saturn occurred six hours after her death. Pluto at 18 Virgo 21 was square natal Saturn; both Pluto and Uranus had been retrograding square Saturn for about a year. Some of the time Saturn had also been square. It had been in Pisces until the March previous to death. Her initial attack of tuberculosis occurred prior to the development of her mental illness. Her bouts of depression and mania likely aggravated it, but her last attack was nearly three years before her death.

Case 12: LBJ's Gallbladder

With the natal Lights, Mars and Mercury, its ruler, in Virgo, Johnson's gallbladder disease may have been infectious cholecystitis, especially with the Sun and Mars both conjunction the Moon. However, Saturn's quincunx to natal Moon and Mercury makes one think of crystallization, gallstones, cholelithiasis. Both are possible, but operations are not usually performed unless there are gallstones. LBJ was operated upon October 5, 1965 (Diagram 31).

His progressed Midheaven at 11 Cancer 31 was separating two degrees from a square to natal Saturn and a semisextile to the Moon, and less than a degree from natal Mercury. Progressed Ascendant was separating one degree from opposition natal Saturn. Progressed Vertex was separating two degrees from square natal Sun; its progressed annual motion was 2 degrees 20 minutes, so it had been exactly square Sun a year and four months previously. Altogether, it appears from these progressions that the gallbladder disease had been going on about a year prior to surgery, with progressed Moon opposition Saturn at that time. (Many astrologers take Saturn or Capricorn, or both, to indicate the gallbladder. I think it is in Virgo as a derivative of the embryological duodenum and that here Saturn is related only as an afflicting natal planet.) Mars also was opposition Saturn 1½ degrees applying.

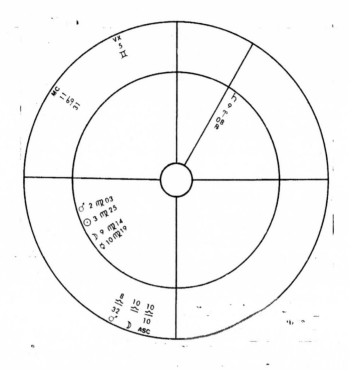

Diagram 31

Johnson's natal Vertex was about 18 Sagittarius. Two days after the operation transiting Uranus and Pluto at 17 Virgo 10 were square the Vertex. Transiting Mars at about 2 Sagittarius 50 was square natal Mars—fortunately for the patient it was separating instead of applying—on the day of the operation.

Going back a year in time, transiting Saturn was in early Pisces, Uranus was in early Virgo, and a year and a half prior to the operation Pluto was also in early Virgo; their periods of aspect to the natal chart coincided with those of the progressions.

As Barbara Watters points out, the astrologer has no control over the competence of a surgeon or hospital staff (29). Moreover, the astrologer has no control over the time when the operation is to be performed and very often no control over the day it will be performed. The most that I have been able to do as a physician and astrologer is advise delay in order for the Moon to pass into another sign on a date later than that scheduled when the surgery is elective.

I could not myself advise the delay of emergency surgery by minutes or hours, unless the surgeon were astrologically oriented and the surgical department also so oriented, so that the surgeon could take my advice. Certainly emergency surgery could not be delayed a matter of days. The astrology might be accurate, but the patient might die.

Watters advises against surgery during all days and hours when the horary strictures against judgment prevail; that is, when the Ascendant is involved, when Saturn is in the first or seventh house, or when the Moon is void-of-course or in the *via combusta*. She advises the avoidance of close quincunxes for heavy planets, especially to the Moon or Ascendant. I advise also against locked-in patterns, such as grand crosses, kites, the yod configuration and other similar ones.

In discussing the *via combusta*. Watters notes that the stars which were in it anciently have passed out of it. Nonetheless, horary charts are invalid when the Moon is between 15 Libra and 15 Scorpio, which she finds to be inexplicable. At least in theory this phenomenon is consistent with the arithmetical zodiac. 0 Scorpio is the lower quincunx (210 degrees) from the life point, zero Aries; anciently sometimes this aspect is associated with death and the *via combusta* in half a sign or 15 degrees orb from that point.

Timing is usually delaying in actual practice. The first thing I advise against is not to operate during the last three days prior to the New Moon because, as in any other project, nothing is finished or done right. The transiting Moon was at about 21 Pisces when LBJ was operated upon, not only not in Virgo but also separated from opposition to the Virgo planets. Had he been operated upon the day before, with Moon at 7 Pisces, the timing would have been less favorable.

Case 13: Joe, Ulcers, Gangrene

Joe is the brother of Esther. Half his natal planets are concerned in his diabetes because they are in fixed signs, and furthermore Pluto is parallel Neptune and square the Midheaven (Diagram 32). Besides his fixed sign oppositions, the Moon is conjunction the Midheaven and opposition Venus in common signs.

In the fall of 1935, Joe sustained a skull fracture at a high school football game. By 1937 he had become so strong physically that he could have been a 'professional strong man; his height was 5 feet 10 inches, his weight was 250 pounds and his chest measured 54 inches. Although recovery from Joe's fracture was uneventful, there had been damage resulting in an abnormal pituitary gland. He elected to become a chemist, however, at which profession he was adaptable and inventive, and was also a good metallurgist. The physical abnormality may have been synchronous with progressed Jupiter's having become stationary direct two years previously.

In 1952, he sustained a fracture of a lumbar vertebra (Libra); Pluto became stationary direct three progressed years before this time. It took a year to heal, which did not slow Joe down any, but he had to sleep in a chair because his bed didn't give him enough support. By then he weighed 300 pounds.

His diabetes mellitus (he did not have the pituitary insipidus type) occurred when his progressed Vertex conjoined natal Saturn during the winter of 1962-63; it had, of course, been opposi-

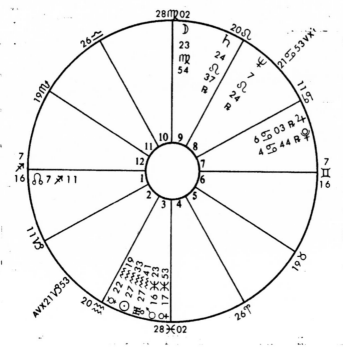

Diagram 32
Joe, February 17, 1919, 1:45 a.m., Medford, Massachusetts

tion Mercury a couple of years previously. Progressed Ascendant was conjunction the Anti-vertex also in 1962-63. From 1960 through 1962, there were many adverse transits to the natal planets in fixed signs.

This section is concerned with Joe's feet. He sustained ulcers on their soles during the winter of 1966-67. In 1970, he lost a toe due to gangrene. He lost two more toes in 1974, and lost the left foot in 1976. He had had gangrene in some toes of the right foot but had not lost any of them. On each of three attacks during the early and mid-1970s his vision failed slightly. After the last two attacks it gradually came back, but after the third attack it came

119

back enough so that he could easily see to get around but not enough that he could read. The last attack nearly killed him because he had septicemia and developed osteomyelitis in a lumbar vertebra, probably the one he had injured years before. In a year he was up and about with a satisfactory prosthesis. In December 1978, the ulcer on the sole of the right foot broke out again, and in early January 1979, cellulitis and then gangrene developed and he lost a previously gangrenous toe. So, for 10 years there were subacute recurrences of gangrene of the toes, and there were ulcers of the soles of the feet for 12 years.

In 1966, the progressed Vertex was at 28 Leo, opposition natal Sun and Uranus. The previous year progressed Jupiter was exactly semisextile Neptune and it was still in orb. The planets are all in fixed signs. The consensus among medical astrologers is that the feet are in Pisces, because presumably it is thought that a neat geometrical plane between the ankles and the foot separate the two signs.

This does not necessarily follow medically. Davidson points out that leg cramps are in Aquarius; these occur primarily in the calves but can also occur due to spasm of the hamstrings on the back of the thigh. But foot cramps are also common, so the muscles of the sole of the foot must also be in Aquarius. Along with the muscles are the bones from which they originate in the same sign. Muscles and bones and motor nerves are all in positive signs; none of these would be in Pisces, a negative sign. There is another medical clue also: The skin over the tibia has very poor blood supply so that ulcers frequently occur on the shins and on or near the inner malleoli of the ankles, which are part of the tibia.

The joints of the foot and ankle are in Pisces. Skin is in positive signs because it is protective of the organism. In insects the outer layer is hard, horny; and there are armored animals. In the human being skin thickens with constant use, producing calluses and corns. Sensory receptors and glands in the skin are in the negative sign following whatever positive sign the particular area of the skin containing the receptors is in.

In Joe's case, because of his weight and the pull of gravity, the subcutaneous tissue broke down and caused the ulcers on the bottoms of his feet. Although only planets in fixed signs were stimulated by progression, it is probable that both fixed and common natal afflictions referable to both Aquarius and Pisces are present in diabetic gangrene of the feet or similar conditions such as Berger's disease and various ulcers.

In 1979, there were four eclipses in Virgo and Pisces, and progressed Venus was square natal Mercury. Transits to malefic planets were heavily aspecting the natal chart.

In 1976, progressed Vertex squared natal Ascendant, and there were the following aspects to Neptune: Progressed Ascendant opposition, transiting Uranus square and transiting Saturn conjunction. A lunar eclipse was square Mercury, and there were two solar eclipses opposition Neptune; one was conjunction Jupiter. The second, October 23, 1976, at 0 Scorpio 04, was conjunction transiting Uranus and Mars in early Scorpio; this eclipse was square Neptune within a few days of the foot amputation.

In 1978-79, progressed Neptune was stationary direct, a lunar eclipse (September 16, 1978) was conjunction natal Moon, transiting Neptune was square the eclipse and recovery was swift and uneventful.

Case 14: Anosmia

On February 6, 1976, this patient came down with a bad cough and had greenish pus in the nasopharynx. The next day she completely lost her sense of smell. There were no symptoms of cerebral infection, so it was obvious that the olfactory receptors

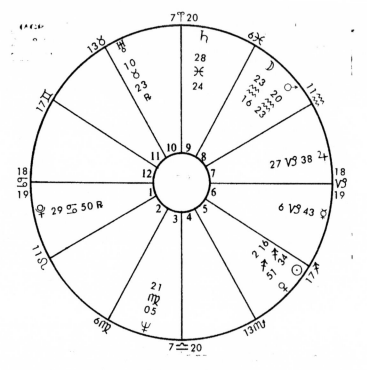

Diagram 33
Case 14, December 8, 1937, 7:17 p.m. CST, New Orleans

in the nose had been damaged. These receptors are under Taurus, and the mucous membrane of that area of the nose is in Scorpio, so the Taurus-Scorpio axis in particular, as well as the fixed quadrature, is concerned.

Note in the natal chart (Diagram 33) that the Moon and Mars are conjunction in Aquarius in the eighth house. Uranus is in the tenth house but so near the cusp of the eleventh house that it may hardly be considered to be in a cardinal house. It can be taken as widely square the Moon if a wider orb is used for the Moon than for other planets; or alternatively may be considered square the Aquarian planets if the astrologer prefers that delineation. Consistent with either delineation is a history of ear infections in childhood and a couple of attacks of severe conjunctivitis. Neptune is quincunx Mars.

At the time of the attack progressed Midheaven was at 20 Leo 06 square natal Mars. Progressed Uranus was at 9 Taurus 44 and was stationary direct the progressed day following; the stationary phenomenon had a strong effect on natal Uranus.

The sense of smell had been lost sometime during the night, and had been discovered in the morning when the transiting Moon reached about 8 Taurus. On the previous January 31, there was a New Moon at 10 Aquarius 30 square transiting Uranus, which was at 7 Scorpio 05. The lunation was widely square the Ascendant of the chart made for the time of its occurrence, at 19 Scorpio 51, square natal Mars. On February 11, transiting Uranus retrograded, so for practical purposes it was stationary on the day of the attack, again an intense effect on natal Uranus. The Midheaven of the lunation chart was at 1 Virgo 52 square Venus, ruler of Taurus, even further augmenting the progressed and transiting Taurus-Scorpio effect.

This case is an excellent example of negative relocation. In the relocation chart (Diagram 34) natal Uranus is .closely square the horizon, and Mars and the Moon are in a cardinal house. The propensity to illness in anatomical areas corresponding with fixed signs had greatly increased.

The sense of smell slowly returned and was almost completely regained three years later, after progressed Midheaven was beyond effective orb of square natal Mars and semisextile natal Neptune.

Of interest pertaining to common signs, this patient developed asthma when she was three years of age, which was severe until she moved to New York state before her tenth birthday. The re-

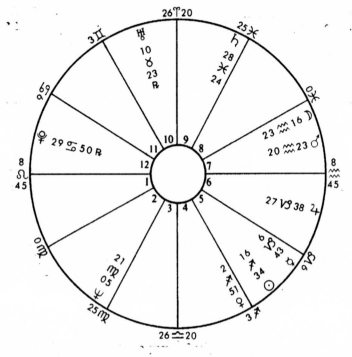

Diagram 34
Case 14, Relocation, 71W04, 41N30

located chart had a Midheaven of 23 Aries 15 and an Ascendant of 6 Leo 30. The lungs are in Gemini, so the common signs are concerned with this anatomical area. The natal stress was on Venus because it is conjunction the Vertex, at 29 Scorpio 34, so that a first-degree proneness existed. The asthma began when the progressed Vertex conjoined natal Venus.

When she relocated, the natal Vertex was no longer conjunction Venus, and the asthma cleared up except for infrequent and relatively mild attacks. Within the year she returned to Louisiana. There was no recurrence of the severe asthma, but this was due to the fact that antihistamines had been discovered.

124

Case 15: Tubercular Arthritis

Despite her habituation to amphetamines, which did nothing to reduce her appetite, this lady was enormously obese; she was a lovely person and an excellent maternity nurse. In 1969, she suddenly contracted massively destructive tuberculosis of the wrist joints (Cancer), the knee joints (Capricorn) and the lumbar vertebrae (Libra). In all three areas both the joints and the adjoining bone were destroyed, and there was permanent malfunction and deformity. Braces were necessary for both knees and the back; despite the deformity she could use her hands. She was in a wheelchair most of the time but was for the most part self-sufficient and could take care of herself.

In her natal chart (Diagram 35) the Moon in Libra is widely opposition the Sun in Aries, and it in turn is conjunction the Vertex. Neptune in Cancer is square Mercury and contraparallel Jupiter. The inflammatory-infectious planets, Jupiter and Mars, are square the Moon. The wrist and knee joint afflictions are consistent with Cancer and Capricorn respectively, whereas afflictions to lumbar joints are consistent with Scorpio. Corresponding positive signs are consistent with the bone destruction.

What is unusual about this case and what makes it relevant to the present subject of common signs is that a latent or subclinical tuberculosis broke out into a systemic infection, so there was a preexistent illness of the lungs (Gemini). (Compare Joe's septicemia related to gangrene, Case 13.)

Progressed Saturn parallel natal Pluto, three minutes separating and in exact orb a year and a half prior to the septicemia is consistent with a flare-up of pulmonary tuberculosis. Progressed Jupiter was parallel natal Neptune, four minutes applying, on her birthday the year of the attack. This is consistent with a flare-up (Jupiter, expansive) without symptoms until the disease was fully developed (Neptune).

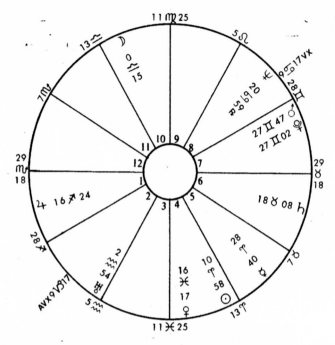

Diagram 35
Case 15, March 31, 1912, 10:00 p.m. EST,
Amesbury, Massachusetts

In 1968, transiting Uranus was square natal Mars and Pluto, transiting Jupiter was square them in early 1969, and transiting Pluto came within orb of square in latter 1969. All were in Virgo, retrograding. There was a solar eclipse opposition her Moon that year, and another one square natal Jupiter; the latter eclipse triggered the septicemia.

Four years later, September 11, 1973, she died of pneumonia. The Full Moon on September 12 was at 19 Pisces; Mercury at 27 Virgo conjoined the Sun. The former planet squared natal Jupiter, and the latter two squared Mars and Pluto in Gemini (lungs) in the eighth house of the manner of death.

VII

Tumors and Degenerative Diseases

The most common degenerative diseases are the arteriosclerosis group, and of these the most common is atherosclerosis. This begins with the deposit of lipids (fatty substances) under the intima (linings) of the arteries, so that plaques form inside the arteries. In some cases the media (middle muscular layer) is invaded, and if this is severe the vessel wall is so weakened that aneurisms occur. (Aneurisms are bulges with thin walls, like an automobile tire ready to blow out.) There may be thrombosis (a clot) of a plaque, and partial or complete occlusion (obstruction of the flow of blood) of the artery. In rare cases part of the thrombus will detach (when a thrombus or piece of it is detached it is called an embolus) and lodge elsewhere. In advanced cases there is calcification.

In some cases of atherosclerosis a chronic inflammatory lesion is simulated. In all cases the disease is slow and insidious and is predominantly one of middle and old age. But "even extensive lesions are not uncommonly found in the coronary arteries in the 20's and 30's" (15).

Atherosclerosis is most common in the coronary, cerebral, and peripheral arteries.

In the coronary arteries their stenosis (narrowing) is the most frequent cause of angina pectoris (literally pain in the chest) due to the fact that the blood supply of the heart is diminished. This is called myocardial ischemia—the myocardium is the heart muscle (Leo) and ischemia means diminution of blood supply, anemia of a particular part of the body. Diminution of blood supply results in lack of oxygen to the tissues. Note that when Eisenhower (Case 8) had his first heart attack there was a relative external lack of oxygen (hypoxia) due to high altitude; myocardial ischemia causes the same effect internally. When it is more severe, there is infarction and degeneration of the heart muscle–in plain language a bit of it dies.

A person may die of a single coronary attack without previous warning, or there may be multiple infarctions producing congestive heart failure, as in Case 9. Or death may occur after two or more attacks, as in the case of Mischa Auer (Case 6). Opposition Leo in Aquarius is the anatomical site of the cardiac pacemakers, and these may be impaired by atherosclerosis. (They may be replaced by electronic pacemakers today, forestalling death.)

The same process, due to thrombosis or hemorrhage (Case 1), occurs in cerebral arteries. Older people usually die of atherosclerotic heart or cerebral artery disease or their complications. Why some people age more quickly than others, such as LBJ compared with Ike, is medically known only to some extent. There is probably an hereditary factor and, in susceptible people, a high fat (more especially saturated) and carbohydrate (especially sugar) diet probably brings out the factor into initial functional disease, which later becomes structural.

128

Diabetics (Taurus) are prone to develop atherosclerosis earlier than are other people. Hypertension predisposes to atherosclerosis, and atherosclerosis predisposes to hypertension or aggravates preexistent hypertension. In the average case the question is whether the egg preceded the hen. Peripheral arterial disease (usually in the lower extremities) is positively correlated with cigarette smoking. Joe (Case 13) smoked a pipe and cigars quite heavily. If the smoke is inhaled, there is a direct arterial effect from the high dose of nicotine. Otherwise the habit is relatively safe in moderation, especially pipe smoking. I have seen both of Joe's legs blanched white, due to arterial constriction. Ischemia (local diminution of blood supply) underlay the ulcers and the subsequent infection and gangrene of his feet. The arteries concerned are in Aquarius. Coronary disease is definitely correlated with arteriosclerosis. Cerebral vascular disease is probably correlated with arteriosclerosis, and nicotine will definitely aggravate it; in high doses nicotine may even cause elevated blood pressure. Tentatively, much atherosclerotic disease corresponds with the fixed quadrature as follows:

- *Taurus*—Diabetes mellitus is associated with earlier atherosclerosis; retinal disease.
- *Leo*—coronary heart disease.
- *Aquarius*—Arterial disease of the legs and feet; aneurism of popliteal artery.

This leaves Scorpio, and this is interesting. The glomeruli of the kidney are arterial and, in Libra, cardinal, are associated with (juxtaglomerulat) endocrine cells that produce renin, which acts as an enzyme to produce angioitensin in the blood stream. This naturally produced chemical is the most powerful pressor (raiser of blood pressure) agent known. There may be an hereditary tendency to overproduction of this substance. Obesity and diabetes are often associated with it. And when there is hypertension, atherosclerosis occurs earlier, as does hypertrophy of the heart and coronary disease. There is a derangement of the sodium metabolism associated with coronary disease, and probably overuse of salt for a long period can precipitate it. Kidney function is often impaired in non-specific hypertension. (There are specific cases of hypertension due to kidney disease, Cushing's syndrome, etc.) Half of hypertensives die of congestive heart failure, and 20 percent die of myocardial infarction so that a total of 70 percent die of heart disease, 20 percent die of cerebral hemorrhage (Case 1), and 10 percent of uremia.

In cerebral hemorrhage and uremia the Aries-Libra axis is involved, so the cardinal quadrature is involved as well as the fixed, statistically in 30 percent of cases.

Much of the cause of the mechanism of atherosclerosis and associated degenerative and functional disorders is unknown, although considerable is known about its details, which appear principally referable to fixed signs in astrology. This is not necessarily because it is a disease of fixed signs, but rather because the heart is more vulnerable. So are diabetics. Second in vulnerability are cardinal signs, and many cases, like Alan Leo's, have fixed sign afflictions as well. Of least vulnerability appear to be organs in common signs; not perhaps because they sclerose less, but rather because they don't wear out as easily. There are cases on record, for example, where 95 percent of the liver (Virgo, Sagittarius) has been destroyed by cancer, yet there was no jaundice because the remainder of the liver still functioned enough that bile did not reach the blood stream. The gallbladder, spleen and small bowel are expendable (Virgo).

The most frequent cases of aneurism due to atherosclerosis are of the infrarenal abdominal aorta, in Libra, again cardinal. The next most common such aneurisms are those of the popliteal artery (Aquarius) and the thoracic aorta (Leo).

These diseases may be categorized as metabolic-aging degenerative conditions.

Even less is known medically about the causes of tumors, or why a certain percentage of benign tumors, for example fibroids or chronic gastric or peptic ulcers become malignant. Certain malignancies are known to be the result of chemical irritation, such as cancer of the respiratory system due to cigarette smoking, and many industrial chemicals are suspect, as well as some food additives. Why certain people develop cancer under the same conditions as other people who do not develop it is unknown. There are degenerative diseases of unknown origin which simply appear comparatively rarely and are neither tumors nor the result of aging factors. Multiple sclerosis is perhaps the best known of several similar degenerations of the nervous system, and there are degenerative diseases of other systems of the body. Some, as for example Tay-Sachs disease and Huntington's chorea, are hereditary. Some degenerative diseases are due to poisoning by heavy metals or solvents. A considerable percentage of the population can tolerate smog, but certain susceptible individuals cannot tolerate it, usually due to respiratory disease.

In tumors and degenerative diseases of unknown (and probably this includes hereditary) origin, Saturn and/or Neptune are usually very heavily involved and aspected, and there is usually a maximal proneness to illness shown in the natal chart. There will be progressions related to the quadrature concerned, and of course adverse transits. Whether Pluto can be a single malefic concerned with malignancy is unknown. I cannot state more specific rules because meaningful research is needed.

By meaningful research I mean the thorough examination of a relatively small (about 20) number of cases wherein the time of birth has been recorded, the pathology is known, and the pathology is in a particular sign. By this I mean that, as in all research, accurate genethliacal charts must be used, and only one specific medical factor must be used and synchronized with the natal and progressed chart in each case. Diabetes mellitus, for example, affects one organ, and one organ only, and produces one illness and one illness only. There are five astrological signatures common to each case studied in the next chapter; their number reduces the probability of error practically to zero, whereas the probability of chance occurrence is multiplied into the millions or billions. If cancer is to be studied, for example, one particular type, for example carcinoma, in one particular organ, for example the uterus, should be studied, and other types of cancer or other organs should be excluded from the study.

Before presenting a few example cases of neoplasm, I have a bit of advice for the reader. When the principles and practice of medicine and its sub-specialties are studied in medical or nursing school, the student comes down with at least one imaginary illness. (I had dengue fever, which doesn't occur in the north.) You may see apparent similarities to the cases discussed in your own natal chart and, may develop astrological correspondences so that a temporary neurosis may develop. The antidote is to go to another astrologer, and also to get a thorough medical examination.

Usually such conditions pass. in a few weeks in medical school. However, my first psychiatric case was that of a fellow student who thought he had had tuberculosis for six months. I simply reassured him and the neurosis passed, never to recur. My first "fee" was collected dramatically when a few years later I developed walking lobar pneumonia which, before antibiotics, was more often fatal than not. My friend may have saved my life with a supply of sulfapyradine he purloined from a hospital where it was used experimentally before it was available on the market. There is also a case on record of a graduate of medical school who developed germ phobia and was unable to practice. He was so phobic that he had to surgically sterilize his eating utensils before meals. The reader will recall the amateur who thought he had cancer of the kidney and needlessly died of uremia (Case 4).

In actual practice, a good case history and the results of a medical examination help pinpoint conditions in astrological terms. The organ or organs concerned are identified as a result, and the sign and quadrature arc determined. In a sense every individual horoscope at a given time is a law unto itself. With both astrological and medical data the medical astrologer in a sense must make certain rules that appertain to the given case. He must, for example, determine whether the slight cardiac distress of today will pass, or whether continuous stress will occur and more possible difficulties will become evident and what these might be. He must determine whether an apparently insignificant benign tumor should be ignored or whether malignancy should be suspected; whether the illness is infectious or degenerative, and what is its probable course.

In the course of practicing medical astrology the practitioner must be prepared to find passing conditions that were not mentioned; to find fully developed and severe illnesses that do not correspond with the symptoms given or with which no symptoms whatsoever were even mentioned. I have had one case with vague symptoms, none of which related to diabetes mellitus, in which I suggested that a blood sugar analysis by made. The astrologer wrote me back that one had been done six months previously. I again suggested a blood sugar test. The patient had diabetes.

About 1975 I had a patient who was due for an operation for gallstones. I suggested a two-day delay because the transiting Moon was in Virgo conjunct natal planets in that sign. She was not operated upon because the stones passed. In January 1979, things were considerably different. She had afflictions in anatomical areas related to all three astrological quadratures. A progressed and transited chart showed relatively minor problems in cardinal and fixed signs, but major problems in mutable signs. Again I advised delay to avoid afflictions to the planets in Virgo. She was operated upon, and this time there was a rarity, a tumor of the gallbladder, but no stones.

The cases that follow are exemplary of tumors. The reader is strongly advised not to generalize any of the particular findings or cases.

Case 16: Mammary Carcinoma

The patient in Case 16 had a right mastectomy January 1974, and a left one August 1977. Except for the skin in Leo and the mucosa in Scorpio, the breast is under the sign of Cancer. In this case (Diagram 36) the cardinal afflictions are in Capricorn and arise with natal Saturn conjunction Mercury; the natal Sun is part of the affliction because it is conjunct Saturn. Both Saturn and the Sun are adversely aspected to all the angles of the chart and are square Uranus, which is in turn conjunction the Vertex.

When the cancer was discovered, progressed Saturn was at 7 Capricorn 24, just three minutes applying to exact square with natal Uranus, and the progressed Moon at 27 Pisces was applying square the natal Sun. For six months prior to the illness, transiting Saturn had been conjunction the natal Midheaven. Pluto had conjoined the ascendant for a year, and the planets conjunction the Nadir; at the time the illness was discovered Pluto was square natal Uranus.

The natal chart indicated more trouble was due, because Saturn, Mercury, Uranus and all the angles are indicative of left-sided illness. Progressed Saturn was still square natal Uranus, separating 18 minutes. Progressed Mercury became stationary direct in progressed year 1975, and is applicable to both illnesses.

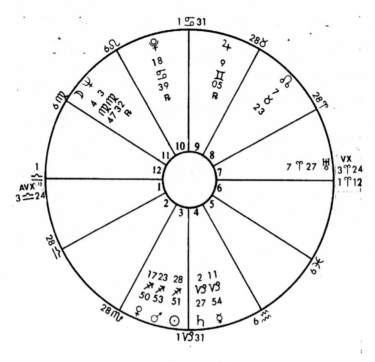

Diagram 36
Case 16, December 20, 1929, 12:03 a.m. EST,
New Bedford, Massachusetts

Transiting Pluto was square natal Mercury; Pluto was conjunction the Moon in a lunar eclipse April 4, 1977. The other breast was removed.

Case 17: Cancer of Uterus

The patient has four angles of the natal chart and a T-square in fixed signs (Diagram 37). Two planets of the T-square are conjunct angles, and a third one is square the Midheaven. The Sun's closest aspect to the other planets in fixed signs is 10 degrees within orb of conjunction Mercury, but the Sun is square the

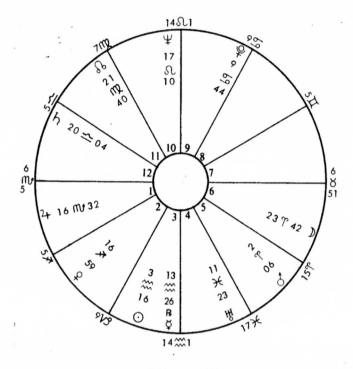

Diagram 37
Case 17, January 24, 1923, 12:55 a.m. CST, Peoria, Illinois

Ascendant.

She was operated upon October 22, 1973, at which time the progressions were few and their orbs wide. Natal Venus at 11 Aquarius 44 was applying a degree and a half conjunction natal Mercury, and natal Mars was separating two degrees conjunction the ascendant. It is probably because the progressions were few that recovery occurred; there was no recurrence by 1978.

The transits were Mars, retrograde conjunction Ascendant, Jupiter retrograde conjunction Sun and Saturn retrograde quincunx Sun. For a year previous to the operation transiting

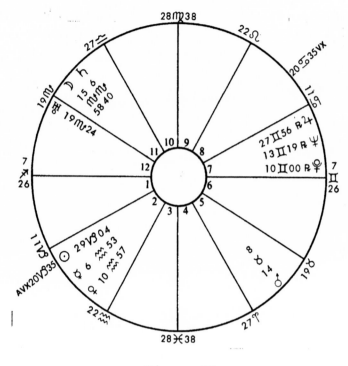

Diagram 38
Case 18

Pluto had been retrograding, opposition Mars, ruler of Scorpio (uterus), and transiting Saturn had been square Mars once and was applying to its second square at the time of the operation.

Case 18: Cancer of the Pancreas, Gallstones

In the summer of 1977 this patient suddenly developed jaundice and pain in the gallbladder region. He was operated upon, and the gallbladder was removed. It had been full of gallstones, and there were no previous symptoms. The gallbladder is in Virgo, in the mutable quadrature (Diagram 38). Note that, of the three natal planets concerned, Neptune (insidious, symptom-free onset of illness) is one of them. Neptune is not only conjunct Pluto but also conjunct Jupiter/Pluto at 18 Gemini/Sagittarius 59, as well as quincunx the Moon. It was also discovered that he had cancer of the pancreas, also in Virgo (except the islets of Langerhans in Taurus), which had also been symptom free, and it was inoperable. This man had eaten enormous amounts of carbohydrates, including much sugar, all his life.

VIII

Diabetes Mellitus
(Sugar Diabetes)

Diabetes mellitus results from the destruction of the islets of Langerhans in the pancreas, so that the insulin they secrete is diminished or absent. As a result there is high blood sugar. The disease begins with an inflamed throat; the patient is thirsty, drinks abnormal amounts of water, and excretes much urine as a consequence. There is usually abnormal hunger, especially for junk foods containing sugar. Diabetics are usually prone to infection and heal poorly.

The pancreas is really a double gland. While it is generally in Virgo as a derivative of the duodenum, the islets of Langerhans are separate anatomically. Since the throat is in Taurus and is first afflicted in diabetes, I ascribe the islets to Taurus. Since the disease begins with an inflammation, afflictions of Mars and/or Pluto should be involved.

Beginning with these presumptions I examined twelve cases for afflictions by major aspect in various signs. In all of them there was a conjunction, square, or opposition in fixed signs by a malefic planet to another planet. In two cases there was no such affliction in cardinal signs, in three cases there was no such affliction in mutable signs, and in one case there was no such affliction in either cardinal or common signs. It was clear that diabetics have as a common feature, afflictions in fixed signs, and do not have afflictions in other signs as a common feature.

This also makes it clear that neither the signs Virgo nor Sagittarius (which appear to rule the liver) are involved; consequently neither are their rulers directly involved. Throughout the literature on medical astrology (such as it is), Jupiter and Venus are associated with diabetes. In three of these cases there were no natal afflictions to Jupiter. In his excellent monograph on low blood sugar (21), Pounds notes that Jupiter and the liver appertained to that illness because the end product of carbohydrate digestion, glycogen, was stored in the liver. This is true because in low blood sugar cases there is an overproduction of insulin with a consequent craving for sugar. The liver is not involved in diabetes, however, because glycogen is not produced due to the lack of insulin. The sugar, which should be stored in the liver, remains undigested by insulin, in the blood stream. Patients with low blood sugar, unless it is treated adequately, may be more prone to develop diabetes, because the insulin-producing cells in the pancreas are continually overworked and cease to function. More than likely certain Jupiter afflictions in diabetes are indicative of prior carbohydrate abuse.

The sign Taurus was not always involved; there were no planets in this sign in five cases. Among these five cases, two of them involved neither Taurus nor its opposite sign, Scorpio. One case had only conjunctions in Leo, and the other had Leo/Aquarius oppositions. Therefore it would be expected that Venus, the ruler of Taurus, would be afflicted. Venus was afflicted by the three major aspects used in all but the tenth and twelfth cases.

While in astrological anatomy the afflicted planets concerned must lie in the quadrature corresponding with the organ involved, the ruler of the sign indicates the physiology of the organ. Anatomically, then, to have an affliction, aspects must necessarily be confined to the three major aspects—conjunction, square and opposition—because these are anatomically locative. Physiologically, I have by experience validated Barbara Watters's conclusion, which she bases on horary, mundane and medical astrology (29), that the quincunx, parallel and contraparallel are major aspects. Since the aspecting planets do not need to be considered as confined to a sign or quadrature as anatomical locators any more than does the ruler of the sign, these aspects are pertinent to the ruler of the sign, as well as influencing planets in other signs.

Case 10 had Uranus, parallel Pluto, contraparallel Venus, and Pluto was also contraparallel to the latter. Case 12 did not have any afflictions to Venus, using the six aspects concerned, and also had no planets semisextile, semisquare or scsquiquadrate that planet. Case 10 had a Leo-Scorpio square, whereas Case 12 had afflicted planets in Taurus. It may be concluded that it' natal Venus is not afflicted, there must necessarily be afflicted planets in the sign of Taurus.

Next, the question of proneness to illness relating to fixed signs was considered. In all cases aspects to angles by planets—conjunction, square and quincunx—in fixed signs were present when the Vertex and the Anti-vertex were used. When only the conventional four angles were used, only seven cases were first-degree prone. The reader who has absorbed the preceding chapters will likely use the Vertex consistently in medical astrology.

As would be expected in nearly any natal chart, there were afflictions by Mars and/or Pluto. However, 10 of these cases had afflictions by Mars and/or Pluto to planets in fixed signs, and one to an angle. Possibly in Case 7 Jupiter, which is conjunction Mercury and square the Moon and Uranus, may indicate infection proneness in fixed signs. In any event she has Mars conjunction Saturn in Aries and cannot wear pierced earrings due to danger of infection. Mars is within four degrees quincunx the Ascendant, more than the orb I use for this aspect and, were the chart rectified, might be in close orb. (She went blind in the left eye in July 1978.)

When the illness was discovered, progressions were noted within a degree of exact orb of planets and/or angles in fixed signs in eight cases. In three cases such progressions were evident when there was an exacerbation of the illness—in Case 2, death; in Case 5, acidosis; in Case 8, coma; and in case 10, hospitalization. In the latter two cases it is unknown whether the disease was first discovered when the patient was hospitalized.

Astrologers seldom do more than pay lip service to (fixed) stars, with the exception of the Sun which is often overdone to the point of the ridiculous. Solstice points (sometimes less accurately called antiscions) are seldom in use except by Uranian astrologers.

Robson (24) has catalogued 110 stars with their exact positions as of January 1, 1920. He includes either one or two planetary attributes, not including the transaturnian planets, summarized from older authors (pp. 108-115). Fifteen of his tabulated stars have attributes of Mars. He does not use transaturnian planets in the table; I have added a sixteenth star, Algol, which appears to have the attribute of Pluto, or of Pluto/Saturn.

Star	Attribute	Longitude
Alcyone	Moon, Mars	28 Taurus 52
Algenib	Saturn, Mars	19 Leo 35
Algol	Pluto, Saturn	25 Taurus 03
Armus	Mars, Mercury	11 Aquarius 37

142

North Asellus	Mars, Sun	6 Leo 25
South Asellus	Mars, Sun	7 Leo 36
Altair	Mars, Jupiter	0 Aquarius 39
Copula	Mars, Mercury	23 Taurus 05
Giedi	Venus, Mars	2 Aquarius 42
Hamal	Mars, Saturn	6 Taurus 32
Khambalia	Mercury, Mars	5 Scorpio 45
Praesaepe	Mars, Moon	6 Leo 07
Regulus	Mars, Jupiter	29 Leo 43
Sharatan	Mars, Saturn	2 Taurus 51
South Scale	Jupiter, Mars	13 Scorpio 58

Ptolemy describes the three Leo stars as "the cloudy spot," which is associated with blindness (22), and which occurs in diabetics even when they are in good control. The Martian, or Plutonic,

as the case may be, influence of the stars is possibly synchronous also with the inflammatory-infectious propensity of diabetics even when controlled. It is a medical mystery as to why controlled diabetics who have relatively normal blood sugars remain prone to infection. It is not an astrological mystery; both diabetics and non-diabetics who have afflictions by Mars and/or Pluto natally are infection prone.

Also of interest are solstice points to fixed stars. There appeared to be a much larger number of them than average in fixed signs which were conjunct or opposition the 16 stars studied. No case had fewer than four planets or angles that were conjunction, opposition, or aspected by solstice to fixed stars.

Watters discusses two of the cases in this study (29) in her book: Cases 5 and 8. I am also indebted to her for case 19 (Diagram 39). She notes that these twins had natal Saturn conjunction Fomalhaut, a phenomenon she has observed in the charts of thalidomide babies. In their natal charts Aculeus also opposes Ve-

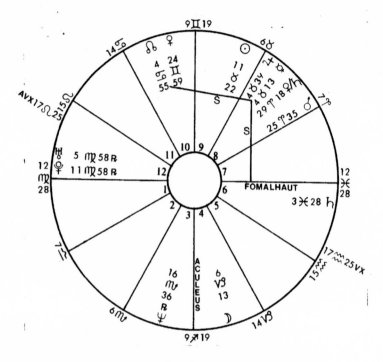

Diagram 39
Infantile Twin Diabetic, May 1, 1961, 1:30 p.m.,
Boston, Massachusetts; twin born 1:40 p.m. EST

nus, which is a Mars (or Pluto) affliction. It is possible that the one twin had congenital diabetes, since the illness was discovered when he was two-and-a-half years old. With an insufficient amount of insulin he may have been able to digest sugar in milk or formula but was not able to handle larger amounts in other foods later. If just slightly less afflicted, and if his diet were restricted, the disease may not have shown up until just before the younger twin's fifth birthday. Had his diet not been restricted, the usual junk foods we feed our children might have brought it out earlier.

In the study of diabetes in the first part of this chapter I did not use Oliver-type midpoints involving Venus. At the outset the first two cases did not have them, and I also think they are physiological rather than anatomical. It is not good research to supply defects in planetary aspects with midpoint configuration, and vice versa, in any series of cases. In the actual delineations of a particular case, however, I think it is good practice to use everything that can be found. In the twins case, midpoints are most significant. Natal Mercury and Jupiter are midpoint Venus/Saturn 29 Aries/Libra 18. When progressed Mars conjoined this midpoint, the younger twin was found to have the illness. Mars was applying within less than two degrees orb when the elder twin was discovered to have diabetes.

I have noted in previous chapters my interest in septiles related to angles and zero degrees in a sign. It is interesting to note that Mercury and Jupiter are conjunct the midpoint on the cusps and are septile both Venus and the descendant of the natal chart. The disease could be genetic in origin. The midpoints of Mars/Mercury and Mars/Jupiter are also very close to 0 Taurus; perhaps the midpoints would not be relevant without the septiles also being there.

Although she was in a paramedical profession, Case 9 did not connect symptoms she had experienced for six months with diabetes until she came out of a coma. On September 4, 1974, at 8:30 a.m. EST her mother took her to the emergency room of a hospital in Providence, Rhode .Island because she was toxic and had a sore throat. Her mother had the presence of mind not to give her the cough syrup prescribed. The sugar could have killed her. Ninety minutes later she was in a coma in a New Bedford, Massachusetts hospital (Diagram 40).

Progressed Jupiter at 4 Scorpio 56 was applying square Saturn at the time, and progressed Moon at 10 Leo was applying conjunction Pluto and square Venus. Progressed Neptune was at 8

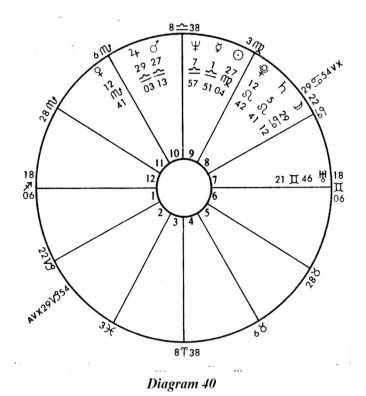

Diagram 40

Libra 59. (If the time of birth had been a few minutes after that given, the conjunction of Neptune to Midheaven would have been exact.) There were no progressions to midpoints associated with Venus, which is conjunction natal Mars. During the six-month period between the onset of the diabetes and the coma, transiting Jupiter, retrograding, was quincunx natal Saturn and Pluto. At the time of the coma Jupiter was at 13 Pisces 10, retrograding almost exactly quincunx natal Pluto. This followed a Full Moon at 9 Pisces, September 1. 'Never let it be said that Jupiter in adverse aspect cannot be malefic. Note in the natal chart the almost exact square between Venus and Pluto. The square between the Moon and Jupiter, with Moon closely conjunction the Vertex, also appertains.

146

Case Data

1. April 25, 1909, 10:00 a.m. CST, Cameron, Missouri. She was discovered to have diabetes in 1968, in which year she also had coronary thrombosis and severe arthritis deformans of the fingers of both hands.

2. December 22, 1911, 41N, 74W, 2:34 p.m. LMT. Died 8:23 p.m. EST, New York City.

3. February 16, 1919, 1:45 a.m. EST, Medford, Massachusetts. Head injury at 16 years of age, after which he became abnormally broad and so strong that he could have become a professional strong man had he chosen to do so. Fractured second lumbar vertebra 1952. Diabetes late 1962. In 1966 or 1967, an ulcer developed on the sole of the left foot. First severe diabetic complication 1970, when he had gangrene and lost a toe. Second flare-up 1974, when he lost two more toes. Developed generalized septicemia summer 1976, with osteomyelitis of the previously fractured vertebra. The left foot was amputated that fall. With each complication he had diabetic retinitis which recovered before 1976. Since 1976, has been unable to read, but gets along well, cares for himself, and walks and drives with the aid of a prosthesis. Good case of remarkable survival type with genius mentality (Chapter VI, Case 13).

4. May 22, 1919, 0:45 a.m. CST, Peoria, Illinois. Diabetes and

hospitalization mid-40's. Nothing more known. Progressions indicate 1945 as year of illness.

5. September 8, 1921, 3:00 a.m. MET, 48N48, 16E20. Severe diabetic acetonuria causing legal problem November 19, 1968.

6. October 2, 1922, 7:45 p.m. CST, Evanston, Illinois. Diabetes discovered November 1973.

7. February 20, K938, midnight EST, New Bedford; Massachusetts. Diabetic since 1955; blind in left eye since July 1978.

8. April 11, 1943, 11:00 p.m. EST, New York City. Diabetic coma May 3, 1972. Alcoholic.

9. September 20, 1946, 12:23 p.m. EST, North Dartmouth, Massachusetts. Diabetes discovered when she went into coma 11:00 a.m. EST, New Bedford, Massachusetts, September 4, 1974.

10. November 18, 1947, 11:32 p.m. CST, Peoria, Illinois. Hospitalized February 12, 1964.

11. May 18, 1955, 10:32 p.m. CST, Peoria, Illinois. Diabetes discovered 1967.

12. May 1, 1961, 1:35 p.m. CST, Boston, Massachusetts. Diabetes discovered at 2½ years of age. Twin born five minutes later. Diabetes discovered shortly before his fifth birthday. Subsequently this paper was presented before the New England Astrological Association, the National Academy of Astrology and the Canadian Fraternity of Astrologers. At the former there was one criticism, that the paper was a postulation and not a theory. I was pleased to learn that an astrologer was familiar with terms of formal logic, but refrained from telling the critic that the paper was a working hypothesis and neither a postulation nor a theory. She suggested six more cases and she was right—the

criticism was more valid than the logic. There was one major change. Among the first 12 cases all of them had a planet in the first decan of a fixed sign, and so did the next five cases. Case 18 had a planet in the first half of a fixed sign but not the first decan, so one signature changed. Although anatomically central, the pancreas derives embryologically from the left side of the duodenum; so this signature is consistent with the Arabic delineation of sides discussed in Chapter IV. The example case used in Chapter III is the only case with a single planet in a fixed sign.

Summary

Of 18 cases having diabetes mellitus, the following astrological phenomena were common to all of them. The first six phenomena are natal.

1. A malefic planet in a fixed sign will afflict a second planet in a fixed sign, or a malefic planet in a fixed sign will afflict two of the three natal axes.

2. A malefic planet in a fixed sign will afflict an angle by conjunction, square or opposition, or it will afflict a planet conjunction an angle by one of these aspects. (The second category of signature 1 is not repeated in signature 2; most cases fall into the first category of signature 1.)

3. Venus will be afflicted by a malefic, or a planet in Taurus will be afflicted. (Except in the infantile, and probably congenital, cases Venus was always afflicted.)

4. Mars and/or Pluto will afflict another planet.

5. A planet will be in the first half of a fixed sign.

6. Four planets or angles will be conjunct, opposition, or solstice within a degree of a star located in a fixed sign which has Martian or Plutonic attributes. (If a star is conjunct one end of an axis it is opposition the other; I count this as two aspects be-

cause the effect is double.)

7. Appropriate secondary progressions were noted in the 16 cases where the onset was known, and they occur with exacerbation of the illness.

Bibliography

1. Carter, C.E.O. "Reminiscences of Alan Leo." *Today's Astrologer*, December 1, 1967.

2. Carter, C.E.O. *Symbolic Directions in Modern Astrology.* New York: Macoy, 1947.

3. Culpeper, N. *Astrological Judgment of Diseases.* Tempe, Arizona: AFA, 1959.

4. Darling, H. F., and Oliver R. H. *Astropsychiatry.* Lakemont, Georgia: CSA Press, 1973.

5. Darling, H. F. *Organum Quaternii.* Lakemont, Georgia: CSA Press, 1968.

6. Davidson, Wm. *Lectures on Medical Astrology.* Monroe, New York: Astrological Bureau, 1979.

7. DeLuce, R. *Complete Method of Prediction.* Los, Angeles: deLuce, 1935.

8. DeLuce, R. *Constellational Astrology.* Los Angeles: DeLuce, 1963.

9. DeVillefranche, M. *Astrosynthesis.* New York: Zoltan-Emerald, 1974.

10. DeVore, N. *Encyclopedia of Astrology.* New York: Philosophical Library.

11. Ebertin, R. *Kosmobiologische Entsprechung.* Aalen, Germany: Ebertin, 1969.

12. Edwards, A. *Vivian Leigh, A Biography*. New York: Simon & Schuster, 1977.

13. Garrison, O. V. *Medical Astrology*. New York: Warner, 1973.

14. Goodman, L. *Love Signs*. New York: Harper & Row, 1978.

15. Holvey, D. L. (eds.). *Merck Manual of Diagnosis and Therapy*. Rahway, New Jersey: Merck, 1972

16. Jayne, C. A., Jr. *Technique of Rectification*. Monroe, New York: Astrological Bureau, 1974.

17. Netter, F. H. *Ciba Collection of Medical Illustrations, Vol. 1*. Summit, New Jersey: Ciba, 1962.

18. Oliver, R. H. *Physique, Temperament and Psyche*. Hollywood, Georgia: Rho,1977.

19. Ostrander, Sheila and Schroeder, Lynn. *Astrological Birth Control*. Englewood Cliffs, New Jersey: Prentice-Hall, 1972.

20. Pottenger, F. M. *Symptoms of Visceral Disease*. St. Louis: Mosby, 1938.

21. Pounds, F. S., Jr. *Seventy-Five Windows*. Tempe, Arizona: AFA, 1978.

22. Ptolemy, C. *Tetrabiblos*. Chicago: Aries, 1936.

23. Raphael. *Medical Astrology*. St Catherines, Ontario: Provoker, 1978.

24. Robson, V. A. *The Fixed Stars and Constellations in Astrology*. New York: Weiser, 1969.

25. Sakoian, F. *That Inconjunct Quincunx: The Not So Minor Aspect*. Tempe, Arizona: AFA

26. Sepharial. *Manual of Astrology*. England: Foulsham, 1962.

27. Silva, J. *Silva Mind Control*. Laredo, Texas: Silva, 1978.

28. Van Norstrand, F. *Precepts in Mundane Astrology*. New York: Macoy, 1962.

29. Walters, B. *Horary Astrology and the Judgment of Events*. Washington, D.C.: Valhalla, 1973.

Glossary

abducens n. Sixth cranial nerve, motor to the muscle of the eyeball which rotates it outward.

acetonuria Urine containing acetone. See ketosis.

achlorhydria Total absence of secretion of hydrochloric acid by the stomach.

acoustic n. Eighth cranial nerve of hearing, also known as vestibulocochlear n.

acute Pertaining to illness, one with a sudden onset, rapid course, and pronounced symptoms.

adrenal gland Also known as suprarenal gland because above the kidney. It is a double endocrine gland. The cortex or outer layer secretes steroids. The inner portion, or medulla, secretes adrenalin.

affect Used as a noun in psychiatry, the accent is on the first syllable. Emotional aspect and feeling tone of a mental state or idea. Sum total of feeling. Sometimes used also as a synonym of emotion.

affective Pertaining to mood, emotionality.

afferent Carrying toward, centripital. In neurology, nerves or pathways which carry impulses toward the cerebrum. Sensory as differentiated from motor. Remember this prefix comes from Latin ad, toward, whereas in efferent the word comes from Latin ex, the opposite. Effectors are pathways going out of, away from, the cerebral cortex, and are more motor than more sensory afferents.

allopathy A system of medicine using remedies that differ from, oppose, symptoms of disease, for example aspirin to lower fever. My medical dictionary (Gould, 3rd ed.) states "It has been applied by homeopaths to the regular medical profession." This latter occurs only rarely because most homeopaths know the meaning of the term (originally propounded by Hahnemann). Osteopathic physicians, however, do confuse the terms as a rule in their literature, equating allopathy politically with the A.M.A.

amphetamines A chemical class of brain stimulants, known as "uppers." Includes Benzedrine, Dexedrine, "speed."

amygdaloid nucleus, amygdala, amygdaloid body If not the seat, the center in the brain most concerned with the fight/flight reaction. It has been removed surgically in cases of severe abnormal aggressivity, also rarely in cases of hallucinations of smell.

anatomy, comparative Sub-science which compares human anatomy with that of other animals.

angiotensin See Chapter VII.

anabolic See metabolism.

anemia Abnormal decrease of red blood cells and/or hemoglobin.

aneurism, aneurysm Progressive dilatation of part of an artery with erosion of the wall culminating in hemorrhage.

aorta The large artery, which carries blood from the heart to the body (except the lungs to which blood is circulated separately by the right side of the heart) from the left side of the heart. The aortic arch curves above the heart and goes down through the thoracic cavity (chest), through the diaphragm and into the abdomen, ending in the pelvis where it divides into the femoral arteries, which supply the lower extremities with arterial blood.

156

Along its entire course are given off major branch arteries.

apoplexy Usually applied to cerebral hemorrhage; sometimes applied to hemorrhage elsewhere but usually under term apoplectiform. Stroke.

arthritis Inflammation of a joint, literally, often applied also to degenerative joint diseases (for which latter the term arthropathy is a bit more precise in one meaning at least). Arthritis deformans is rheumatoid disease of the joint. There are many other types of joint disease; arteriosclerotic due to age, gouty due to metabolic disturbance, and rheumatic arthritis are most common.

articulation In anatomy, the junction of two or more bones or skeletal parts, including fibrous and cartilaginous joints. Moveable joints are called synovial joints as a class, and immovable ones are synarthroses; there are several sub-classifications.

asthenic Physical type which is slender, flat-chested and angular, with poor muscular development, and often introverted.

asymptomic Symptomless.

atherosclerosis, arteriosclerosis See Chapter VII.

auditory n. Acoustic n.

autonomic nervous system This is also known as the vegetative or sympathetic nervous system. Generally speaking, it may be said to control involuntary bodily functions over the entire body, such as sweating and change of color of the skin (and in animals the raising of hair), the regulation of the entire digestive system from digestion in the stomach to defecation from the rectum, the expansion and contraction of blood vessels, automatic breathing and the heart beat.

"Sympathetic nervous system" as a term applied to the entire autonomic nervous system is archaic but is still used occasionally. The term applies to half—the more active half—of the autonomic nervous system, which, when it is comparative, overactive, gives rise to the physiological term sympathicotonia, which means that the body is put into a fight/flight reaction; the blood vessels contract, there is gooseflesh, muscle tone increases, the blood pressure rises, the pulse and respiration accelerate. The sympathetic branch is composed primarily of ganglia at each spinal segment, one on each side of the spinal column, so that there are two chains, one on each side of the spinal cord; parallel to the cord; the sympathetic cords are sometimes equated to the Ida and Pingala of tantric yoga. (In the first place they are not anatomically equivalent, are not cords that extend from the occiput to the coccyx as usually described as for instance by Woodroffe in *The Serpent Power*, for above and below the thoracic area the ganglionic nodes become plexuses as described in Table 5, Chapter I. In the second place they may be in the body's Kirlian field or aura and not anatomically related exactly.)

Sympathetic stimulation resembles the effect of an injection of adrenalin, and indeed if sympathicotonia results from great anger or fear the adrenal medulla releases this neurohormone into the body.

Not only is this adrenal gland intimately connected with the sympathetic nervous system but so is the limbic system, the upward extension of the sympathetic system into the brain through the medulla oblongata (oblong middle part, literally) which is the direct extension of the medulla spinalis (spinal cord) within the skull, into the more primitive, premammalian, parts of the brain particularly in the optic hypothalamus, which may be described roughly as the seat (but not necessarily the cause) of emotion connecting with some nuclei there and extending forward to the amygdaloid nuclei, which relate directly to fight/flight. This complex is sometimes called the "cerebral sympathetics."

Oppository to and balancing the sympathetic nervous system is the other division of the autonomic nervous system, the parasympathetic or craniosacral system. Overstimulation of this system is known as parasympatheticotonia or more simply as vagotonia. Referring again to Table 5, Chapter I, note that except for some fibres from other cranial nerves and the pelvic nerve, which supplies parasympathetic innervation to the urogenital system, the parasympathetic nervous system equates with the tenth cranial or vagus nerve (except for a few of its motor fibres).

The sympathetic system aids catabolism, the expenditure of energy, motion, extroversion, whereas the parasympathetic system aids anabolism, the storing up of energy and quietude of the body.

Note that the lungs are usually under involuntary (autonomic) innervation but that breathing can be voluntary (motor). The heart is ordinarily involuntary. These and other autonomic functions can be put under a certain amount of voluntary control by various methods varying from autohypnosis (including yoga) to biofeedback.

Relative to anatomy are also the seven etheric centers (or chakras). As in the case of Ida and Pingala there is probably no direct correspondence between these biomagnetic foci and the anatomy of the human body, although certainly there must be some connection or indirect correspondence. By this I mean to say that the solar plexus is a part of the human body which relates to and corresponds with, but is not identical with, the navel (or manipura) chakra, for example. Relating to chakras anatomically, there is no such thing as the splenic chakra; I believe this was invented by puritanical Theosophists to avoid mention of sexual terminology. The chakras are from below upward: root, gonadal (not splenic), navel, heart, throat, brow and crown. (One modern author uses both splenic and gonadal chakras complicating matters .even further.) A full discussion in *The Serpent Power* relates to what East Indians think, not to what Anglos say they think, about tantric yoga.

In passing I must note that *Tantra: The Yoga of Sex* by Omar

Garrison is not the tantric yoga described in either *The Serpent Power* or in Evan-Wentz's *Tibetan Yoga and Secret Doctrines*, both of which scriptures are in the bibliography of Garrison's book. Real tantric yoga is individual, psychological and, as far as sex is concerned, only symbolic of the positive and negative polarities of the conscious and unconscious. Garrison's method may be entirely valid, really East Indian and greatly therapeutic for psychosexual problems (hopefully more valid than his medical astrology) or it may not; I do not necessarily criticize the method but rather the title is misleading.

The relationship between the sympathetic nervous system and the adrenal glands has been noted. In general there is an interrelationship between all the endocrine glands and the autonomic nervous system. Despite systemic attempts by astrologers and others to equate one endocrine with each zodiacal sign it just doesn't seem to work that way in practice. This is perhaps because the nervous system (including the endocrines) is incredibly complex.

bifurcation Division into two branches, or the site of this division.

bilateral On both sides, as for example the kidneys. Its opposite is unilateral, on one side, as for example the spleen

calcification Mineralization of tissue with calcium.

canals, semicircular This is a system of tubes in the inner ear which are partly full of fluid. When the head moves so does the fluid, and consequent nervous impulses orient the body to position. This is the mechanical-neuronic part of the body's balancing system.

capsule A membrane surrounding a part or organ of the body. In movable joints the capsule is attached to both bones and surrounds the joint.

carcinoma A form of malignant tumor, or cancer.

cardiac Pertaining to the cardium, or heart.

cardiac decompensation Failure of the heart by over-stretching the muscle.

cardiac dilatation Enlargement of the heart by over-stretching the muscle.

cardiac hypertrophy Enlargement of the heart muscle by over-development or overuse.

cartilage Gristle. It is like bone but contains no calcium.

catabolic See metabolism.

caudad In direction from head toward the tail.

cavitation The formation of an abnormal space in tissue by disease or injury.

cecum The large, blind pouch from which the colon (large intestine) begins. The (vermiform) appendix is attached to it. (If the reader is not a physician, remember that "appendix" is *singular* and should be referred to as "it," not "they," especially around physicians—and indeed around high school graduates if properly educated. Plural is appendices or appendixes, the latter most used in England.)

celiac plexus Solar plexus. From this plexus the splanchnic and vagus nerves supply the abdominal viscera or organs.

cell salts These are twelve mineral preparations in homeopathic concentration developed by Schuessler and are a subdivision of homeopathic medicine rather than astrology. Since there are several dozen homeopathic mineral preparations, and the twelve cell salts do not coincide with the chemistry of cells and especially of intracellular fluid, their proper and safe use would be only as homeopathically indicated.

cellulitis Diffuse inflammation of connective tissue, especially subcutaneous, according to my medical dictionary (Gould, 3rd ed.). In practice, cellulitis is infection of the skin and subcutaneous tissue with redness, swelling, pain, and fever—as the term is commonly used, not only inflammation.

cephalad Toward the head; opposite of caudad.

cerebellum Postero-inferior part of the brain, below cerebrum and above pons.

cerebrum The largest portion of the brain occupying the whole upper part of the cranium (skull), consisting of the right and left hemispheres. (Literally the cerebellum means "little cerebrum" and it too has hemispheres.)

cervical ganglion (plural **ganglia**). There are two of these, superior and inferior, and sometimes a third, middle, ganglion in the sympathetic chains of the neck. There is also a cervical ganglion at the uterine cervix and this is parasympathetic.

cervix Like appendix this word is singular, not plural. It means neck, or constricted portion. Most commonly it refers to the "neck" as used in ordinary English, which is between the head and thorax, and also the lower constricted portion of the uterus.

cholecystitis Inflammation of the gall bladder.

cholelithiasis Gallstones.

chronic Long-continued. Compare acute.

ciliated Hairy. Pertains to the eyelashes and also, as used in this book, to describe membrane which has fine moveable threads or, in fancier language, ciliated epithelium "in which the cells bear vibratile filaments or cilia on their free surfaces" (Gould).

cilium Eyelash or thread. Plural cilia.

cirrhosis Destruction of cells with hardening (fibrosis) by connective tissue. Usually term is applied to the liver but it can refer to tissues other than liver.

clavicle Collar bone. It extends from the breast bone to the upper/outer tip of the shoulder where it joins with the acromial process of the scapula; that is, the extension of the shoulder blade to the upper/outer tip of the shoulder. The clavicle and shoulder blade join here in an immovable joint which is known as the claviculo-acromial joint (or acromioclavicular).

cloaca In lower animals and the early embryo an undifferentiated organ related to excretion. Renal and intestinal excretion are differentiated in later development.

coccyx The last bone of the vertebrae column, below the sacrum, formed of four rudimentary vertebrae which are fused.

cognitive Adjective of the noun cognital. Awareness of thoughts and perceptions and ability to reason pertaining to them.

colitis Inflammation of the large bowel.

colon Large bowel. The adjective is colonic.

coma Unconsciousness from which arousal is not possible.

complication An accidental and/or secondary disease occurring in the course of a primary illness. For example, pneumonia occurring during influenza is a complication. See sequela.

conception Fertilization of an ovum by a spermatozoon.

congenital Existing before or at birth, or dating from but not necessarily detected at birth.

conjunctiva Mucous membrane covering anterior (front) portion of eyeball and lining the eyelids.

contraception Prevention of impregnation.

cornea Transparent anterior portion of eyeball.

coronary Adjective from corona, literally meaning garland, and referable to any encircling vessel. Specifically, relating to the heart, the coronary arteries originate from the aorta and supply the myocardium (heart muscle). If this supply is interrupted and as a consequence part of the heart muscle is damaged, this is known as a coronary attack or disease. There can be a spasmodic contraction of a coronary artery often known as angina or angina pectoris (literally pain in the chest). A branch of a coronary artery can be occluded, obliterated, or there can be a thrombus (clot) in an arterial branch, or an embolus (detached clot from elsewhere in the body) can lodge in a branch, or coronary stenosis occurs, which is narrowing without complete blockage.

corpus luteum An endocrine body which develops in the ovary during pregnancy.

cortex External layer of an organ; if the organ has a capsule, the external layer
beneath the capsule is meant.

corti An organ pertaining to balance. See "canals, semicircular"). Corti worked out detailed anatomy in this area.

cortico-cortical Relative to the cortex of the cerebrum, this term relates to the transmission of impulses between the cells within the cortex, making normal cognition possible. See cognitive.

cortico-thalamic Relates to transmission of impulses between the cerebral cortex and the hypothalamus, making normal integration of cognition with emotional impulses possible.

costovertebral Joints between ribs and vertebrae.

cranial nerves Those nerves which originate in the brain and supply other organs; necessarily they must, in their courses, pass through holes (foramina) in the skull.

cranium Braincase, skull with or without (more commonly) mandible

Cushing's syndrome Adrenogenital syndrome. An endocrine illness due to various causes and having various variations in sexuality as the result of hormonal disturbance, including adrenocortical disfunction.

decumbiture Literally, taking to one's bed, but can mean the time an illness begins.

degeneration Partial or complete destruction of cells or organ (can also mean progressive mental, physical, or moral deterioration of a person). Often means progressive chronic deterioration, particularly when the term "degenerative disease" is used or implied in context.

dermal Pertaining to dermis; layer of skin below the epidermis. Cutaneous.

diabetes When unqualified, means diabetes mellitus, sugar diabetes; see Chapter VIII. Diabetes insipidus also is characterized by excessive thirst and consequent excess of urine but is not due to inability to utilize sugar.

disc, disk Circular plate-like organ or structure. Refers usually to intervertebrae discs which are between the vertebrae, are made of cartilage, cushion the vertebrae, and are contained in the joints between the vertebrae. Meniscus, plural menisci as well as disc, is more often used to describe the cartilages contained in the knee joints than is disc.

duodenum First 8-10 inches of the intestine beginning at pylorus of the stomach and into which the pancreatic and bile ducts enter.

duodenal bud A bump on the primitive duodenum of the embryo from which an organ later develops.

dysplastic Adjective from dysplasia, abnormal development or growth. As used in describing somatic types (general bodily types) it means a type differing from normal asthenic, athenic, or pyknic types (which see).

eclectic Combination of various schools of medicine with elements selected for their utility. Also a system of herbal medicine, as a separate school of medicine which existed until comparatively recent times; homeopathic pharmacies still sell the tinctures used in eclectic medicine and some homeopathic and regular physicians still use them. The eclectic school had origins in both European and Native American herbal medicine; the latter is still extant.

ectoderm The outermost of the three embryonic layers, which gives rise primarily to the skin.

ectomorphic type A physical type in which the nervous system is emphasized. See asthenic.

effector Motor or secretory nerve which ends in an organ, gland, or muscle.

efferent Carrying or conducting away. Compare the opposite, afferent.

embolus A bit of matter foreign to the bloodstream (clot, cells, fat, cluster of bacteria, foreign body) carried by the bloodstream which eventually lodges in and obstructs a vessel.

embryology The science of the embryo and its development.

emphysema Destruction of air cells in the lungs.

endemic Native to a region or people; refers to a disease which is more or less constant in a given area or among a given people. See epidemic.

endocardium The membrane lining the heart. The valves of the heart develop embryologically from the endocardium.

endocrine glands Those that secrete directly into the bloodstream as contracted from those that secrete otherwise usually by ducts (exocrine).

endoderm The inner of the three embryonic layers which forms the linings of the gut from pharynx to rectum, and its derivatives. Also entoderm.

endomorph Soft, round, viscerally predominant physical type. Same as pyknic type in original classification of types.

enteritis Inflammation of intestinal tract, particularly of small intestine.

epidemic Extensive outbreak of a disease.

epidemiology The study of the occurrence and distribution of diseases.

excoriation Abrasion of portion of skin, often severe or marked.

facial nerve This is the seventh cranial nerve and is motor, sensory, and parasympathetic in function.

fauces The space between the soft palate and base of the tongue. The other tissues surrounding it are known as the palatoglossal and palatopharyngeal arches

fertile Prolific, fruitful

fibrillation Uncoordinated muscular twitching. As related to

166

heart muscle it means very rapid irregular, non-coordinated contractions.

fibroid Composed of fibrous tissue. Any fibrous tumor. Usually describes a type of non-malignant growth or tumor.

fibula The smaller bone of the leg. Begins just below the knee on the outside and ends at the outer, external malleus, which is the roughly hemispherical bony bulge above the ankle; the inner malleus is the end of the tibia or shinbone.

fontanelle Membranous space between cranial bones in fetus and infant. Known as "soft spot" at birth in plain English.

gangrene Death of part of body with putrefaction.

gastric Pertaining to the stomach.

gastritis Inflammation of the stomach.

genito-urinary or urogenital The organs of the body including both the sexual and urinary system.

gingivitis Inflammation of the gingiva or gums.

glans penis The erectile body at the distal (further) end of the penis.

glaucoma Describes a group of diseases which are resultant from increase of pressure within the eyeball.

glomerlulus Tuft of capillary loops; the glomerluli comprise the vascular part of the kidney.

glossopharyngeal nerve The ninth cranial nerve. It has motor, sensory, and parasympathetic components; supplies parts of pharynx, ear, mastoid.

gonorrhea A venereal disease producing primarily infection of the genitourinary tract and can produce secondary septicemia with arthritic, cardiac and/or meningeal complications.

glycogen Sugar stored in the liver; it is utilized by insulin the lack of which produces diabetes.

hemoglobin The respiratory pigment of the red blood cells, called respiratory because it can take up oxygen. Hemoglobin is red when oxygenated and blue when it is not.

hereditary Inherited. It may also be congenital if it is apparent at birth, for example six digits instead of five, or may appear later in life like diabetes, for example.

homeopathy A system of medicine which uses specially activated minute doses of medicine prescribed primarily according to symptoms and secondarily according to diagnosis of disease.

Huntington's chorea A hereditary disease of the nervous system characterized by onset in adult life of purposeless bodily movements, disturbed speech, dementia, and eventually paralysis and death.

hypertension High blood pressure.

hypertrophy Enlargement of an organ with concomitant increase in its function.

hypogastric nerve This is a sympathetic nerve arising from the superior hypogastric plexus, a branch of which forms the pelvic plexus. Supplies sympathetic and visceral sensory impulses to pelvic viscera.

hypoglossal nerve Twelfth cranial nerve, motor to tongue.

hypotension Low blood pressure, the opposite of high and NOT anemia which is diminution of red blood cells and/or hemoglobin.

hypothalamus Part of the brain below the cerebrum, relates to certain cranial nerve nuclei and those related to emotions.

ilium The superior broad portion of the hip bone.

infarction A localized area of dead tissue resultant from insufficient blood supply.

infection Invasion of organ or entire body by germs.

inflammation Reaction of tissues to injury, with heat, swelling, redness and pain. Infection can produce these same symptoms but the cause is different. (I note that my medical dictionary [Gould] defines these terms properly but confuses them in other parts of the dictionary.)

infrarenal Below the kidney.

insertion See origin.

insidious Literally deceitful. Onset of illness gradual inappreciable symptoms.

intracranial Within the skull.

intracellular Within a cell.

intercellular Between cells.

internal carotid nerve A sympathetic nerve which forms plexuses on the internal carotid artery and its branches. This artery supplies much of the brain.

intima Innermost of three layers of blood vessels.

ischemia Local diminution of blood supply; localized tissue anemia.

ischium Inferior part of hip bone, that upon which one sits (no relation whatsoever to ischemia).

islets of Langerhans Ductless, endocrine glandular areas in the pancreas which secrete insulin and a hormone related to liver function.

jaundice Yellowness of skin, conjunctiva, and secretions due to liver dysfunction.

juxtaglomerular Next to a glomerulus.

katabolism Catabolism. See metabolism.

ketosis Excess of ketones, a type of chemical including acetone, in the body due to diabetic and other acidosis.

kinesthesia Sense of perception of movement, position, weight and resistence to bodily movement.

labyrinth See canals.

lacrymal Pertaining to tears and the organs which secrete and convey them.

larynx Voice box.

ligament Band of flexible tough tissue connecting two or more bones. There are also certain visceral ligaments.

limbic system See autonomic nervous system.

logorrhea Excessive abnormal uncontrollable loquacity. Figuratively: diarrhea of words.

lumbar Pertaining to the loins. Low back between rib cage and sacrum.

lumbosacral Pertaining to lumbar vertebrae and the sacrum

lymph The clear fluid in lymph vessels.

lymphatic Pertaining to lymph. As noun, a vessel containing lymph.

malignancy Refers to malignant tumors, those which grow progressively and endanger life—cancer. Malignant as adjective refers to any condition that endangers life

malleolus See fibula.

mamma Breast; mammary, pertaining to breast.

mandible Lower jaw bone.

mandibulotemporal or temperomandibular Pertaining the joint between the lower jaw and the temporal bone of the skull.

mastectomy Removal of breast.

maxilla Upper jaw bone.

media Middle coat of a vessel. (Also plural of medium).

medulla oblongata Most caudal part of brain from pons to spinal cord, an upward extension of latter.

medulla spinalis Spinal cord.

membrane Thin layer of tissue surrounding a part, separating cavities or adjacent structures, or lining a cavity.

    ciliated m One with microscopic hairs on free side.

    erectile m One that swells.

    mucous m One in contact with air which keeps itself moist by secreting mucus.

    serous m One lining closed cavities, has flat cells and watery surface.

meninges (plural of meninx). The membranes that cover the brain and spinal cord.

mesial Medial. Toward the middle.

mesentery A fold of peritoneum that connects the intestine with the posterior abdominal wall.

mesoderm The middle of three embryonic layers, from which derives connective tissues, muscles, and the urogenital system.

mesomorph Athletic type. Sthenic type of habitus—body build, appearance and extroverted personality.

metabolism The phenomena of synthesizing food by the body into complex substances, known as assimilation or anabolism; plus the phenomena of breaking down these complex substances into simple ones, known as dissimilation or catabolism.

metastasis Transfer of a disease from a primary focus to a distant one by means of the circulatory vessels; refers both to germs and abnormal cells, infection and cancer respectively

mons pubis Eminence of lower abdominal wall above the pubic bones.

motor Action due to muscular movement. Innervation, by efferent nerves, of muscles.

muscle A tissue composed of contractile cells. There are three types: smooth, involuntary and unstriated (unstriped); voluntary, striated; cardiac; branched, striated, involuntary.

musculoskeletal Pertains to skeleton, muscles, and joints

myocardium The heart muscle.

nasopharynx The space behind the choanae (posterior nostrils) and above a plane through the lower margin of the palate.

nephritis Inflammation of kidney.

nephrosis Degenerative disease of kidney

neural groove In embryology a structure from which develops the brain and spinal cord.

neuron Complete nerve cell. Adjective neuronal.

nucleus Central body of a cell. Also a collection of neurons concerned with a particular function.

oculomotor nerve The third cranial nerve, which innervates most of the muscles that move the eye.

olfactory Pertaining to the sense of smell. The olfactory nerve is the first cranial nerve.

optic Pertaining to the eye. The optic nerve is the second cranial nerve of sight terminating in the retina, which is the organ of sight.

origin The beginning, usually referable to the beginning of nerves in their nuclei and to skeletal muscles. The origin of skeletal muscles is in the cephalad of the two bones concerned, whereas their insertion is in the caudad, or more distal bone.

osseous Adjective of os, bone; bony, bonelike.

ossicles Small bones. Refers particularly to those of hearing; the malleus, incus, and stapes—hammer, anvil, and stirrup-which relate to the eardrum.

osteomyelitis Inflammation of marrow and hard tissue of the bone; bone infection.

Paget's disease There are three of them: 1) Cancer of nipple and/or areola of breast, and larger ducts (referred to in this book) 2) Osteitis deformans, a disease of the skeleton with simultaneous osseous hyperplasia (overgrowth of bone) and deossification, resultant in skeletal deformity 3) A type of skin cancer.

pancreas See chapter VIII.

parasympathetic See autonomic nervous system.

parasympathicotonia See autonomic nervous system.

parathyroids Endocrine glands situated near or sometimes imbedded in the thyroid gland. They relate to calcium metabolism; their deficiency or absence produces tetany.

patella Kneecap.

pathology The study of the nature of disease. Laboratory findings related to a disease.

pericardium The closed membranous sac which covers the heart.

peripheral Outer, near surface.

peritoneum Serous membrane which lines the abdominal cavity and surrounds the contained viscera.

pharynx Muscular tube covered with membrane situated back of nose, mouth, and larynx, above and continuous with the esophagus (gullet).

phobia Abnormal or abnormally intense fear or aversion. Adjective, phobic. Its opposite is *philia*, abnormal craving, used as a combining form only. Phobia is used separately and as a combining form.

phylogenetic Pertains to the evolutionary history of a biological group or species from the simplest form. (*Ontogeny* is development from fertilized egg to adult without evolutionary implications).

pineal body or gland. A ductless gland which becomes atrophied at puberty. At roof of third ventricle of brain.

pituitary gland Hypophysis. Endocrine, gland which lies in sella turcica of sphenoid bone and is attached to the third ventricle. It is functionally a double gland with many different hormones and quite often is characterized as the master gland of the endocrine system. It is intimately interconnected with the autonomic nervous system.

placenta Afterbirth. It is an organ which exists during pregnancy which is attached to the inner uterine wall and attached to the embryo by the umbilical cord, by means of which the embryo is nourished.

pleura Serous membrane which lines the chest cavity and envelops the lung; it is double and normally lubricated. When infected, the resultant disease is called pleurisy.

plexus A network of interlacing nerves or of interconnected blood or lymphatic vessels.

pons A convex white eminence at the base of the brain; consists of fibers and nuclei which connect with cerebrum and cerebellum.

popliteal space Diamond shaped area behind knee.

portal system Abdominal veins which are interconnected with the liver, draining eventually into the vena cava, and the latter into the heart.

prepatellar Situated in front of the kneecap. The prepatellar bursa when infected and enlarged cause the familiar condition known as water on the knee or prepatellar bursitis in medical language.

proprioceptive Pertains to sensory receptors located in muscles, tendons, joints and the organ of balance in the ear. They make possible the kinesthetic sense, which see psychosis Impairment of personality and/or mental function to the point that there is gross interference with the ability of the individual to function in his environment.

psychosomatic Pertains to mind-body relationship as to afflictions which have both emotional and bodily components, or bodily complaints of mental cause. Psyche is mind, soul, or self. Soma is the physical body.

pubis Portion of pelvis in front, below abdomen medially to ilium.

puberty The period of adolescence during which the sexual organs become capable of reproduction.

quadriceps femoris muscle So named because it has four heads of origin in pelvis; it covers the front portion of the thigh and inserts into the tibia, below the kneecap. The tendon of insertion contains the kneecap.

receptor cells These receive sensory impulses from all the sensory which are transmitted to the brain along afferent, sensory nerves.

renin A hormone related to high blood pressure.

respiratory Pertaining to respiration, breathing. The lower respiratory system is the lungs, trachea, larynx whereas the upper respiratory is the nose, sinuses and related structures.

reticular system A network of nerve fibers and cells related to motor and sympathetic nervous system function situated in the lower parts of the brain.

retina The organ at the back of the eye which is the end of the optic nerve and contains receptors of sight.

retinitis Inflammation and/or infection of the retina.

rheumatism Can be synonymous with arthritis which is generalized but more often related to rheumatic fever.

rhinitis Inflammation of the mucous membrane of the nose. Dry rhinitis is an atrophic inflammation and/or one due to low humidity.

root, nerve Bundle of nerve fibers that emerge from the central nervous system. Spinal nerve segments have anterior and posterior roots.

saphenous veins External veins of the lower extremities which often become varicose. Veins to lower extremities are double and saphenous veins can be removed but the deeper, femoral, popliteal and tibial veins cannot ordinarily be removed.

schizophrenia A form or forms of introverted psychosis.

sclerosis Hardening, particularly by fibrous tissue. Especially applies to degeneration and fibrous invasion of the nervous tissue in a group of diseases of undetermined cause, the most common of which is multiple sclerosis. Also applies to arteries; for .arteriosclerosis, see Chapter VII.

sensory Pertaining to or conveying of sensation.

septicemia Severe infection of entire bloodstream.

sequel or sequela A disease that follows another one, as differentiated from a second related disease that arises during a primary disease. See complication.

sesamoid bones Those small bones which develop in tendons that are subjected to much pressure. The kneecap is the only sesamoid bone which is always normally present in the human being.

shoulder girdle The system of bones supporting the upper limb-clavicle, scapula and upper sternum.

sign Objective evidence of disease. That which the physician sees, feels, or hears as opposed to what the patient describes, which are symptoms.

somato-motor Tracts having to do with muscular innervation.

somato type Body type, can include personality types associated with major body types.

spasticity A state of muscular spasm.

sphincter A muscle enclosing and surrounding an orifice, allowing for opening or closing it either involuntarily or at will.

(spinal) accessory nerve The eleventh cranial nerve which supplies some muscles of the shoulder girdle.

sthenic type Athletic type; one of Kretschmer's original body type terms; mesomorph.

stenosis Constriction or narrowing of a lumen, orifice, or value of the heart, as for example mitral stenosis.

sternum Breastbone.

sternoclavicular joint That between the breastbone and collarbone.

subacute Intermediate between acute and chronic, both of which see; also is used to refer to a subsequent outbreak of acute illness which broke out previously and became latent.

subclinical A disease so slight or insidious as not to be noticeable.

subdermal Hypodermic; beneath or below skin.

suprarenal gland Adrenal gland.

suppressor area Area of cerebral cortex which suppresses motor response of some other area of the cortex. Also known as suppressor band.

sympathetic nervous system; sympathicotonia See autonomic nervous system.

symptom What patient feels due to disease.

synarthrosis A joint which is normally immobile.

syndrome A particular group of symptoms and signs which together characterize a type of illness or disease.

Tay-Sachs disease Familial idiocy with associated blindness; infantile amaurotic familial idiocy.

temporal lobe syndrome Violent paroxysms of rage which are epileptic; equivalents, originating from the temporal lobe of the cerebrum. Since condition was discovered it has been found to relate particularly to certain nuclei in the limbic system. See autonomic nervous system.

tendon The fibrous end of a muscle which inserts in a bone, particularly in wrist and ankle surrounded by a sheath. It is not a ligament; ligaments are not : parts of muscles and connect two or more bones testis, plural testes Male reproductive gland.

thoracic Pertaining to the thorax.

thorax The chest, not including the shoulder girdle.

thrombus A clot formed in a blood vessel or the heart.

thrombosis Formation of a thrombus or thrombi.

tibia The larger leg bone. Shin bone.

tissue salts See cell salts.

tonus Degree of contraction present in skeletal muscle. If diminished, the muscle is flaccid; if normally increased, it is spastic.

trace element Elements essential to health and life but present only in very small amounts in the body.

trachea Windpipe.

tract Pathway or course; usually refers to nervous pathways of brain and spinal cord which are anatomic and functional entities.

trigeminal nerve The fifth cranial nerve, so called because it has three branches, one to each jaw area and one to the upper face.

trochlear nerve The fourth cranial nerve which supplies an eye muscle.

tumor An abnormal mass due to the excessive multiplication of cells; classified roughly into benign or non-cancerous, and malignant types.

uterus The womb. Uterine pertaining to the womb.

ureter Tube between kidney and bladder.

urethra Tube by which urine is discharged from the bladder and excreted.

vagus nerve The tenth cranial nerve. See autonomic nervous system.

vascular Consisting of, containing, or provided with vessels; pertaining to vessels.

vegetative nervous system See autonomic.

venous Pertaining to a vein or veins.

venous sinus A vein like a canal or chamber. (Nothing to do with the bony sinuses of the face and head).

ventricle Pouch. Particularly applies to the two venous chambers of the heart—the other two are auricles—and the hollow areas in the brain which are filled with spinal fluid.

vertebra A single bone of the spinal column. Plural vertebrae more common than vertebras.

vesical plexus Refers to an autonomic nerve plexus surrounding the vesical artery. (There is also a venous vesical plexus about the lower part of the bladder and prostate gland).

vestibular In neurology, relates to equilibrium.

vestigeal Pertains to a remnant or trace of something left over from something more fully developed. The appendix, for example, is a vestigeal organ phylogenetically speaking.

viscus, plural **viscera** Any organ within one of the four great bodily cavities—cranium, thorax, abdomen, or pelvis: especially an abdominal organ.

visio-auditory Pertaining to both sight and hearing.

visual purple, also known as **rhodopsin** A pigment contained in the rods of the retina, preserved by darkness and bleached by light.

unilateral One sided; on one side of body.

urogenital Genitourinary.

urogenital diaphragm Sheet of tissue stretching across the pubic arch, formed by the deep transverse peroneal and sphincter urethrae muscles.